— Exeter in the 1940s —

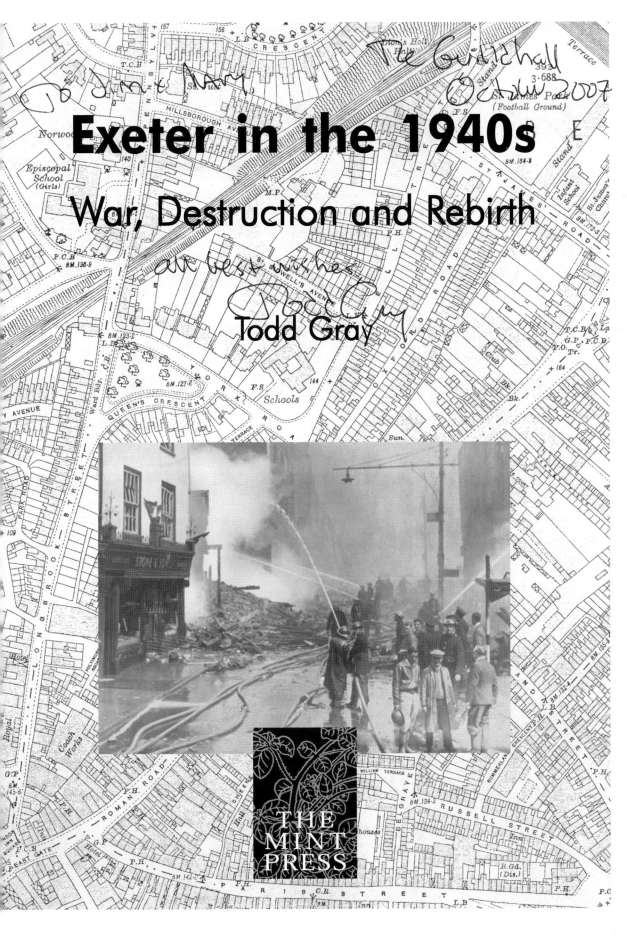

Exeter in the 1940s

War, Destruction and Rebirth

Todd Gray

THE MINT PRESS

First published in Great Britain by
The Mint Press, 2004

ISBN 1-903356-39-3

Cataloguing in Publication Data
CIP record for this title is available from the British
Library

The Mint Press
18 The Mint
Exeter, Devon
England EX4 3BL

Designed and typeset in Futura 10.5/14 by
Mike Dobson, Quince Typesetting

Cover design by Delphine Jones

Printed and bound in Great Britain
by Short Run Press Ltd, Exeter

— Contents —

— Acknowledgements —

I would like to thank all of those who contributed their memories of the 1940s in Exeter. Paul Cleeve, Graham Parnell, Maurice Pike and Dick Passmore have kindly contributed very useful material. Permission to publish illustrations has been given by the copyright holders. I would also like to thank John Draisey, Devon County Archivist, for his help with documentary references and Tony Rouse of the Westcountry Studies Library for assistance with newspaper and secondary sources. Finally, Professor Andrew Thorpe has considerably improved this book with many useful comments. Any and all remaining errors are of course my own.

— Foreword —

Exeter's years during the second world war are among the most important in its long history. Even now, some sixty years later, we still refer to the war as a key reference point. It dramatically changed our city in a great number of ways and yet we still do not have a comprehensive history.

I welcome this book which tells us so much more. It will remind those who lived through these years of the city's everyday life and inform those who were born afterwards of the importance of the second world war.

I warmly recommend this book to you,

Councillor Hilda Sterry
Lord Mayor of Exeter

For Sharon & Richard

— Introduction —

The 1940s, more than any other decade in the twentieth century, altered the city's landscape — in those years it went through war, destruction and rebirth. We have to go back three centuries, to the Civil War, to find another period with as much destruction and reconstruction. Yet, even though these are extraordinarily important years, there are great gaps in our knowledge and it is unlikely a complete story will ever be told. There are three main reasons for this. First, official censorship of the press limits the usefulness of newspapers: details were often not reported because they might prove useful to the enemy. Secondly, few people in official posts had the time or inclination to record events at the time. All effort was needed to win the war, not record it, consequently council minutes are not informative. In 1942 Mayor Roland Glave Sanders asked his chief officers for their personal accounts. Only James Whiteside, the city's Emergency Information Officer, wrote a report[1] and the mayor was so discouraged by the response he himself did not write one. Finally, few ordinary people recorded the war at the time and since then there has not been a concerted effort to gather together memories and keep them in a publicly accessible place. It is hoped the creation of an archive at the Devon Record Office will help to correct this. But a great deal of time has passed since the war and each year there are fewer people with memories of the 1940s.[2] The result is that there are some completely unknown aspects. For instance, it is said in the months leading to war Sir Oswald Mosley's Fascists gave public addresses on weekend nights outside the Civic Hall and at the end of Sidwell Street. Nothing has been recorded of who these individuals were, what their numbers were and whether they were subsequently incarcerated. Were they significant in Exeter? It is unlikely we will ever know.

This book pieces together in a monthly form Exeter's main events in the war and summarise the efforts made to rebuild in the late 1940s.[3] Oral histories will help to fill some gaps but the greatest contribution this book makes is in using the city's civil defence papers. This is the first time this important collection has been used in print. These several thousand documents were deposited in 1962 and contain extraordinary details of events. A substantial number were marked 'confidential', 'secret' or 'most secret'.

Exeter in the late 1930s had a mix of Victorian, Georgian, Early Modern and Medieval buildings with a sprinkling of more modern styles. There was some light industry but it was much less industrialised than even nearby Plymouth. One visitor described it as having 'a large, tame population of movie-goers; a handful of upper-crusters, not so tame; a good library; no music to speak of; and a rather distressing preoccupation with entertaining and being entertained . . . The main street itself is narrow, swarming with traffic, and lined with hunched-up buildings three or four stories high. Occasionally the round-shouldered ranks of commercial architecture are interrupted by an old Tudor façade, slanting, insecure and quaint, with projecting upper floors'. Another visitor in the 1930s saw prosperous shops filled with London's fashions and largely unconcerned with its past.[4] By 1931 there were just over 66,000 residents but Exeter has been described as being relatively quiet. The University College of the South West was growing and there were hopes that one day it would become a university. There was identifiable social change with the council's work on slum clearance, tramways ended in 1931, automobiles were becoming more common and national chain stores gradually replaced local shops.[5] In 1939 it was fairly prosperous and ancient in its character. Few could have guessed how it would fare over the next six years.

Four themes are of particular interest for Exeter: these are the course of the war in the city, evacuees, the civilian war effort and reconstruction.

THE WAR IN EXETER

War was declared on 3 September 1939. Exeter, like the rest of Britain, had been anticipating it for several years. It was as early as 1936 that the

1. *C. J. Newman (left) with F. Willey of the National Fire Service.*

city prepared for war: on 27 July that year the mayor chaired a meeting of the Special Committee regarding Air Raid Precautions. One point they discussed was whether the military would use local school buildings.[6] Roland Glave Sanders was mayor through the war but the pivotal figure was Cyril James Newman, town clerk, and, more importantly, in charge of civil defence as air raid precautions controller. He remains something of an enigma. Newman was appointed in 1930 and at age 30 was the youngest to serve as town clerk. He was prominent but not universally liked and he had sharp disputes with Exeter's chief constable, librarian and fire officer. Among the stories about Newman was that he stood on the north tower of the cathedral at the blitz contemplating rebuilding. But did he really shout 'Come on, burn! Just think of the rateable values'? Newman was awarded an OBE in October 1942, remained in office until 1961 when he retired in ill health and died in 1973.[7]

The key event was the bombing in May 1942. Five books have been written on it with one published shortly after it happened.[8] There are also two analyses of the reconstruction of Exeter.[9] It is a testament to the importance of the blitz that anyone who lived through it still clearly remembers what he or she was doing at the time.

Intense preparations were made for the possibility of bombing although many residents, and even some local authorities, did not expect it would happen. In the first few months Exeter was thought of as a safe city. Six hundred civil servants were sent from Whitehall as well as hundreds of

2. Holloway Street after a daylight raid.

schoolchildren, many of whom came from London, Middlesex and, later, Bristol. As late as February 1940 it was promoted as a 'haven in which to relax'. However, the suddenness of the French defeat in spring 1940 caused a rethink. German planes along the Channel were close in proximity and there were serious concerns of bombing and invasion for some time after. Some Whitehall staff were withdrawn from Exeter in these months but other evacuees, particularly children, were increased. Civil servants decided it was safe for children but less so for their own colleagues. The 'winning' of the Battle of Britain in autumn 1940, the German attack on the Soviets in June 1941 and the Americans entering the war in December 1941 made it less likely the Germans would invade. In Exeter though there were still warnings of invasion throughout 1942. There were also continued concerns over bombing through to the Normandy landings in June 1944 and with the sudden use in London of the V1 flying bombs and V2 rockets.

In Exeter the first bomb fell in August 1940 but the most serious bombings were from 23 to 25 April and on 4 May 1942. These last attacks were 'Baedeker Raids', retaliation for the attack by the R.A.F. on Lübeck in late

(opposite) 3. The city centre as it was in 1932.
Mr Vincent began his journey from Coombe Street.

March. On April 14 some of England's most beautiful cities (Canterbury, York, Norwich, Bath and Exeter) were selected from the German tourist guide. For most of the war the city authorities expected gas would be used in an air attack. There was extraordinary planning including, in one instance, distributing 36 pails of bleach cream to pharmacists as an antidote against blister gas.[10] But when destruction came it was caused by some 75 tons of high explosives and 10,000 incendiary bombs. Casualties were high: 273 died and a further 732 injured. Some 1,734 buildings were destroyed while approximately another 18,849 were damaged.[11]

An extraordinary account was written by Reginald Vincent, a 34 year-old resident of 21 Cowick Road:

In the early hours of Monday morning May 4th I proceeded to Tan Lane to collect Rescue Lorry immediately on the sounding of the Alert. From Tan Lane I went to West Street to switch off pumps which were working over an unexploded bomb from a previous raid. Proceeding through Coombe Street to South Street just as bombs fell, which forced me to turn back, and up through Palace Gate to High Street. Bombs falling in High Street forced me to turn into Queen Street so I proceeded along Blackall Road where the railway siding had started to burn owing to incendiaries, two of which fell on the lorry which I immediately removed without damage or injury, and proceeded on my way up Longbrook Street, where I was again forced to turn back by buildings which were already well alight. By this time I was so alarmed I really did not know which way to go, but believe I must have gone down Longbrook Street and through York Road, where again all buildings were burning fiercely. As I turned into Sidwell Street a bomb dropped on a public shelter about 15 yards in front of lorry, at this point I noticed a woman with two young children, very upset having apparently

lost her house and was shouting for her husband. I managed to get them into the lorry thinking to take them to safety at the depot. The debris from the bomb crater had blocked my way, so once again I took the only way out, and retraced my way back into York Road, where what I believe to be an oil bomb dropped alongside us, & proceeded up through Pennsylvania, and across Union Road, down into Mt Pleasant Road turning into Monks Road, where once again a bomb dropped immediately in front of me at a distance of between 30 – 40 feet, which caused great discomfort to myself and passengers, owing to my driving into edge of crater. The difficulties removing lorry from debris, coupled with my anxiety for my passengers, possibly accounts for the time taken to cover this comparatively short distance. Once again I went on, turning back through Monks Road, and down into Pinhoe Road, the screaming of my passengers caused me to look through the window at rear of cab to see if they were alright which forced me to slow down, the incident I believe, being responsible for me being able to write this report, as a bomb dropped immediately in front at a distance of 20 ft, the blast of which threw the lorry at right angles to the road, also blowing or throwing my passengers from the vehicles. On searching I was not able to find them, and the lorry now being completely surrounded by debris I was forced to cover the last few hundred yards to the depot on foot, arriving approximately 10 minutes before the 'All Clear'. We were then sent to Mowbray Avenue, particulars of this rescue working [party] having already been supplied by W. Parsons, leading hand, No. 5 Squad Rescue Party.[12]

His supervisor later wrote 'This man is one of my Yard Charge Hands and a mechanic of considerable skill. He is a member of a Rescue Party and also acts as the driver of the lorry. His actions on the night of 3rd – 4th May show a particular devotion to duty and a disregard of his personal safety in face of danger.' He supplied further details including that Vincent's passengers fled apparently unharmed from the lorry.[13]

After the bombing there was immediate criticism of the local authorities although it is difficult to gauge how effective or efficient they were. Certainly individuals made tremendous efforts amid overwhelming destruction. There was some panic: at 2 pm on the following afternoon a bulletin of the Emergency Information Service urged 'no able-bodied man nor any person capable of dealing with an Incendiary Bomb should leave his home or City to the mercy of the Enemy at night'. Thousands left to sleep in safety in neighbouring villages and fields. On the next day the service announced 'It has been reported that a rumour is current in Whipton that all children are about to be evacuated from the district. There is no truth whatever in this rumour. No arrangements for a general evacuation of children are being made or are being thought of. Please deny this rumour whenever you hear it'.[14]

Fuller details of the attack are given in the pages below but it is interesting to note here the almost casual remarks made immediately afterwards by the town clerk to his counterparts throughout the country. He wrote to Wandsworth 'Poor old Exeter had a nasty knock, but everyone has been splendid' while to Plymouth he noted 'We certainly had a nasty time, although small in comparison with yours and as you say, after a few quiet nights the problems begin to solve themselves. Everyone has worked splendidly and we have had the greatest assistance from all our neighbours'. He also made a fascinating comment to his Coventry counterpart: 'I am sorry to say that a large section of our High Street has completely disappeared, and except for a small portion, the old world charm has disappeared for ever. Our total deaths for the three raids in April and May was 261, including missing, and I quite agree with you that the number of killed in all cases which I have heard seems surprisingly low having regard to the nature of the attack. I too wonder whether the same does not apply to our bombing in Germany.'[15]

Were the city authorities prepared? It is interesting there is only one account from a key city figure. In 1942 James Whiteside recorded his experience and provided illuminating details of local preparations:

This is my personal story. I was appointed Emergency Information Officer in the early months of 1941: my sole qualification for this work apparently being that I was already Honorary Secretary to the local Committee of the Ministry of Information. I was also at that time adjutant of the Exeter Battalion of the Home Guard. I gave this up.

At the time of taking over the work of the Emergency Information Officer the period of intense air attacks on England was at its height and it seemed certain that Exeter sooner or later would be singled out for a heavy raid. My large duties were defined for me very simply: my task was to sustain public morale in what was described as a 'blitz aftermath' – just that!

I prepared what I dubbed 'The Emergency Information Service Operational Scheme': I enlisted a few friends, members of an organisation of which I was President, and together we rehearsed the scheme. The difficulty with which we were faced in rehearsal was, of course, the sheer impossibility of reproducing artificially anything like the conditions under which we would be likely to work, even if we had known, otherwise than in imagination, what these conditions would be. The scheme was designed so as to give every man a 'key' job – something of his own which he would engage himself upon without seeking instruction or advice.

The scheme and the team then went into cold storage, to emerge from time to time for further discussion and for further recruitment of volunteers. In October 1941, with Mr Haley (Deputy City Treasurer), I prepared an eighty-page Handbook of Emergency Information. Publication was held up due to difficulties in getting paper supplies, but in March 1942, the handbook went to press and 3,000 copies were produced. These were distributed among police, civil defence workers, doctors, clergymen and all people who could be regarded as leaders of any group within the city, with the exhortation in the preface that 'each would become an information officer in the moment of need and, before that moment arrived, would be a fountain of accurate knowledge within his own circle'.

And the scheme and the team remained in cold storage. I had looked at the scheme; talked about it; added to it; subtracted from it; even, at the request of the Ministry of Information, addressed conferences upon it; forced, against my inclination, into the limelight as an expert upon a subject of which I knew exactly nothing that was not born of imagination. As the months went by, and as my expectation that Exeter's turn was fast approaching was sharpened, I ceased to be fearful of life or limb in an air raid: but I began to be haunted by fears for my reputation in an aftermath. Would the scheme work? I did not know. By this time I had come to have grave doubts about it. With my team I went through the scheme again on the afternoon of Sunday, 20th April 1942.

In the following week there were three nasty raids. The scheme was not brought into operation, but some members of the team gained a little experience in loud-speaker announcing in areas that had been affected.[16]

Whiteside's booklet became known as the Blitz Bible. His description of the blitz and how effective his plans were appears on pages 76 to 81.

Another is that of Reverend Phil Pedrick who was at the Catholic Church on South Street. On 8 May he wrote:

We are not on the phone – lines down. Pat Magill is evacuated to Topsham Senior School because of unexploded bombs at hospital. They were delighted to see me at Topsham still in one piece.

Your letter came this afternoon – our first post. Included was a priority telegram from Ed (Buckfast). The G.P.O. must have thought we were gone as the envelope said 'House Burnt' – not yet thank God thought it would seem so as all South Street is burnt down but for our church and house and the Baptists next door. We fought hard to keep God's house and attribute our safety to the Sacred Heart and His Holy Mother. Fires came down our side of the street right to the corner house, with the wind our way. Embers showered all over us, and the old sand-bags in the tower caught fire. Our poor legs – we were up & down. We plastered our house roof with sand and also the top of the tower, then pumped water all over the front of the house and church to keep things cool. When all the houses opposite were on fire the heat was fierce and melted our paint and buckled some of the lead in the West Window. Our doors were scorched and blinds & window frames stuck hard with the heat. Early in the morning another scare came – fire was coming from behind us near the Deaconess, it broke out again in the afternoon but was put down. All South Street is down but a few houses on our little block may be repaired, but I doubt it.

Palace Gate had fire licking their wall but it stopped there. First they ran to get all our books down from our rooms & then had to go over to see to their own home. Truly, the centre of Exeter was ablaze. Parts of High Street, Fore Street, Bedford Circus, Southernhay, are burnt as is the City Hospital & St Luke's College. Heavitree presbytery is down and Rosary House School is damaged. The church house is badly knocked and the tower unsafe. A bomb skimmed the tower before landing on the presbytery. All are safe there. They hit a chapel of Exeter Cathedral and we got all the debris – we thought we had been hit. Bombs here very close to us, even in our street.

My view is lovely now, all across Haldon.

We have had some meals at Palace Gate to relieve Miss Jane, so much dirt and want of gas is a bother but we have electric and a fuel stove. Father Barney stood up to the ordeal very well.

He added as a postscript 'three Catholic servants were killed at a colonel's house. Casualties are few from our point of view but many homes in parish are damaged'.[17]

After the bombing the city had intermittent attacks and altogether there were 19 raids. Nearly 300 died, thousands of buildings were damaged and nearly 2,000 destroyed.[18] It was almost exactly three years after the blitz, on 7 May 1945, that Germany surrendered. Exeter vigorously celebrated VE Day, and a few months later, VJ Days. It took many years for the city to rid itself of reminders of the war and for a while it appeared that civil defence could be revived with a threat perceived by the Soviets. The mayor summarised the war in December 1944 as being 'long periods of extreme dullness punctuated by brief spells of danger and excitement'.[19]

The Civilian War Effort

While the city's men and women in the armed forces were fighting abroad there was also a tremendous effort back in Exeter. At the start there were 2,345 men and women in civil defence. In June 1940 the number of wardens increased from 41 to 175 and there were 94 shelter wardens. Four years later it was even higher: there were 1,266 general wardens (excluding fire-wardens) and 74 shelter wardens. There were also 248 men in the rescue services, 102 in decontamination and 91 messengers. The war effort included a great number of others including the home guard and the land girls. Some branches were more popular than others.

Women made a great contribution to Exeter's war effort. It was dependent upon them. Yet, at first there were discussions on whether women should be employed in various occupations and if they should continue when war ended. Interestingly, in June 1943 there was a great debate on whether women should have permanent contracts. One councillor argued very strongly that women were just as capable as men. The role of the Women's Voluntary Service, founded in 1938, was particularly exemplary. Moreover, they were so useful the women could not resign their positions at the end of the war. They argued they had signed up to help win the war, not to continue during peacetime.

Allotments were another great issue in the city. In September 1939 there were discussions on increasing public provision and this continued through the war. The council also planted crops in a number of public places including parks. By 1942 the national number of allotments had increased to 1,450,000 from 815,000 in 1939.[20] At one point there were more than a thousand allotments in Exeter and many grew vegetables and fruit in private gardens.

Evacuees

More than ten thousand evacuees came to Exeter. There were several different types: some were officially sent from other parts of the country, notably London, Bristol, Kent and Middlesex, and others came privately. Many were children and some mothers came with them. Several hundred people with little or no sight were also brought to Exeter and there were a considerable number of civil servants from London.

Not all evacuees were welcome. In the autumn of 1939 Exeter's Chief Sanitary Inspector noted common complaints from hosts ('indolence of mothers and entire absence of control of toddlers', 'unclean habits of children – beds, carpets, furniture and floors being constantly fouled', 'fleas brought by evacuees', 'neglect by some mothers of their personal cleanliness; slovenly habits e.g. soiled napkins left under bed', 'reminder by evacuees that she is paid for looking after them', 'allowance under Form A insufficient for hefty school boys') but there were also comments from the evacuees ('taken in good class houses, conditions are too good, dislike of servants', 'constantly locked out from morning till night', 'veiled abuse and open resentment by some occupiers', 'difficulties made in the matter of access to cooking facilities').[21] One complaint came from Mr Baseter of 21 Danes Road, a six-roomed house in which he and his wife lived. His letter reveals the difficulties of mixing people of apparently different classes. His concerns were a 'child 2 years old, destructive, unclean habits. Mother does not control him. Bed being ruined through wetting. Mother low-class Cockney. My wife's health is being affected through worry. She has got into a nervous state. I'm afraid she is going to become ill. These people should all be housed with families like themselves, people who are rough and ready'. But the next day he wrote 'I had occasion to complain to you yesterday about Mrs Hughes and family, evacuees from London, who are staying in my house. I spoke sharply to her on Wednesday night about the boy's behaviour and dirty habits, also to her lack of control over the boy. There has been a vast improvement since. I now wish to withdraw my complaint and give her a chance to go on improving. I realise we have to be patient and help all we can to improve these people. If the mother will cooperate I am sure the little boy can be taught to be clean in his habit. My wife has made the mother wash all clothing belonging to the children.'[22]

One particular story about the blitz attracted great interest across the country. The *Daily Mail* reported about three orphans of the blitz and readers from Fakenham, Lyme Regis, Newcastle, Caernarvon, Brighton, Sheffield, Retford, Bicester, Watford and Henlow, among others, wrote offering to adopt the children.[23] The story was, however, inaccurate. It is interesting there was a great deal of goodwill towards orphans created by bombing but not always towards evacuee children.

The city hosted 'blind evacuees': in the first few months of the war more than 200, including eight soldiers, were sent to Exeter. The West of England Institution for the Blind had been in St David's Hill since 1838 and during the war a further 118 blind men and women from London and Middlesex were evacuated to the city. They were employed making baskets, knitting and repairing shoes. Until 1943 the Royal London Society for Teaching and Training the Blind also had workshops at Palace Gate and Allhallows church. Like other evacuees, those with impaired sight were not always wanted. One Exeter official stressed the problems and thought some needed to try harder to retain their hosts' goodwill. He also encouraged them to find voluntary billets 'for the sake of their own happiness' but noted in Exeter people willing were 'very few indeed'. Records show at least 67 offers of accommodation were made in Exeter: one resident of Townsend Cottages wrote 'I am willing to do my duty for our country in time of war. I could take one child of school age, but if possible would help a blind female to live with us, as we could make a canopy bed in the kitchen'.[24]

Some stories are moving if not heart-rending: Mrs Elizabeth Kingscott, was evacuated to live at 59 Roberts Road: she was born in 1853 and at the age of 88 was not only visually impaired but noted as 'suffering from senile decay, is mental and quite helpless'. There was also Mrs Elizabeth Caroline May Fairchild. Her Southampton home was demolished by bombing and arrived with her husband, their two sons and a daughter who was just over one year old. Mrs Fairchild had been without sight since the age of 24, had previously been institutionalised for mental health problems and upon arrival in Exeter, where she and her family were housed in an unfurnished basement, gave up her youngest child for adoption.[25] Many others had escaped bombing in London and found refuge in Exeter. Perhaps the strangest story involved Mr Albert Prince Heasman, who was evacuated from London. His coming to Exeter elicited an extraordinary letter of 7 September 1943 from Mr J. J. Johnston, a tax inspector of 195 Pinhoe Road, to the Chief Billeting Officer.

Dear Sir, I beg to report that the above named has been living at my house for about two months. He came apparently on the invitation of my wife and without any permission from me. Some months ago my wife made his acquaintance and he occasionally called at the house – she began walking out with him and I found her neglecting her domestic duties. As time went on he began having more or less regular meals at the house. Eventually I walked in from work one evening about two months ago to find a number of boxes etc. in the passage. I asked my wife who they belonged to and she replied 'Mr Heasman, he is

Copy

195 Pinhoe Road, Exeter
7th Septr. '43.

re Mr. Heasman,
Blind Evacuee,from London.

Dear Sir,
    I beg to report that the above named has been living at my house for about two months. He came apparently on the invitation of my wife and without any permission from me.
    Some months ago my wife made his acquaintance and he occasionally called at the house - She began walking out with him and I found her neglecting her domestic duties. As time went on he began having more or less regular meals at the house. Eventually I walked in from work one evening about two months ago to find a number of boxes etc in the passage. I asked my wife who they belonged to and she replied Mr. Heasman, he is going to live here. I answered "he is not", but for the man being blind and for the scene that would be created I did not take any desperate action. As a matter of fact he was sleeping two nights in the front sitting room before I was aware of the fact. He did not have the ordinary decency to see me and ask if I was agreeable. - Since he has been here I feel that I am worse than a lodger as my wife is neglecting me and continually walking out with Heasman . They dine together when I am at work and are very often out together when I arrive home. I have to meet all expenses and feel I am suffering from neglect. The reason I am putting this case to you is that I cannot and will not continue to live such conditions. I am in a Government position and have a deal of writing to do at home. The man sings & whistles loudly in the house and is very disturbing when one is trying to concentrate. Under the circumstances may I request you to remove Mr. Heasman from my house and if possible from the City, because even if moved only from the house my wife would still carry on with him.
    I shall be obliged if you can help me in this matter otherwise further domestic complications may follow. Thanking you in anticipation.

Yours faithfully,
J.J.Johnston.

Mr.Robins,
8 Southernhay W.
Exeter.

4. This letter by J. J. Johnston expressed his unwillingness to host a blind evacuee.

going to live here'. I answered 'He is not', but for the man being blind and for the scene that would be created I did not take any desperate action. As a matter of fact he was sleeping two nights in the front sitting room before I was aware of the fact. He did not have the ordinary decency to see me and ask if I was agreeable. Since he has been here I feel that I am worse than a lodger as my wife is neglecting me and continually walking out with Heasman. They dine together when I am at work and are very often out together when I arrive home. I have to meet all expenses and feel I am suffering from neglect. The reason I am putting this case to you is that I cannot and will not continue to live with such conditions. I am in a Government position and have a deal of writing to do at home. The man sings and whistles loudly in the house and is very disturbing when one is trying to concentrate. Under the circumstances may I request you to remove Mr Heasman from my house and if possible from the City, because even if moved only from the house my wife would still carry on with him. I shall be obliged if you can help me in this matter otherwise further domestic complications may follow, thanking you in anticipation.

In the months that followed Mrs Johnston's mother and blind father interceded to remove Mr Heasman. Because the house was in the name of Mrs Johnston and her father there was little Mr Johnston could do. The Billeting Officer also tried to remove Mr Heasman. He failed but was able to stop his state allowance. Finally, in the spring of 1944 Mrs Johnston informed the relevant authorities that Mr Heasman's financial support should still be sent to her address and noted her husband had left the household in October 1943. The town clerk then interceded to have the Ministry of Health cut Mr Heasman's funds. It refused despite the assertion of 'feelings of disapproval in blind welfare circles'. Interestingly, Mr Heasman was then aged 56, had lived in at least three other billets in Exeter from 1939 to 1943 and had a wife and three adult children in Middlesex. Mrs Johnston ran her own business from home as a 'Spirella Corsetiere'.[26] It seems extraordinary that in the midst of wartime the case merited the considerable amount of staff time.

In addition to schoolchildren and evacuees with little or no sight, some 600 civil servants were secretly living in the city. Because of censorship little was recorded about them other than the buildings requisitioned. The city also hosted some Dutch and Belgian evacuees.

RECONSTRUCTION

During the Christmas Season in 1943 the mayor said 'We have made a start with the re-planning of Exeter and I feel sure that we are going to decide to leave High Street much as it has been for so many years'. Two years later Thomas Sharp was appointed to draft a plan to rebuild the city and unveiled his work in 1946. Temporary accommodation for housing and retail were sought immediately after the main bombing. Housing was planned from at least February 1944 and built in 1945 whereas retail buildings were erected as early as 1948. A great deal of the future shape of Exeter was planned at this time but the majority of the building took place in the 1950s and 1960s.

5. Boy dispatch riders of the National Fire Service.

The bombings in spring 1942 had destroyed a great portion of the city centre and presented opportunities for modernising Exeter. The initial destruction and subsequent rebuilding drastically changed the character. Throughout the planning there was a considerable amount of public discussion as to what shape it should take and subsequent unease at the plans. It was recognised that the reconstruction was the largest that had taken place in the centre for hundreds of years and every aspect had its supporters and detractors. Interestingly, these discussions began whilst the war was still being fought and some sixty years later the results of that debate are still being discussed. The 1940s closed with the visit by Princess Elizabeth to officially mark the building of Princesshay and the recent public debate over the demolition of that development is part of this long debate stretching from the mid-twentieth century into the twenty-first. The second part of this book examines how the reconstruction plans were discussed and decided. It is commonly said in Exeter today that the city planners in the post-war period continued the destruction of the city initiated by the Germans. In particular it is pointed out that many historic buildings were unnecessarily demolished. This view was based on the experiences of those who lived during the 1940s and passed on to subsequent generations. There has been no documentary evidence shown to back these views. However, the account of the reconstruction given below reveals for the first time the view of the country's Inspector of Ancient Buildings: in 1942 he singled out Exeter's council as being responsible for the 'worst case of vandalism' in the country he had seen.

The war brought with it a great number of government initiatives with the result a bewildering range of abbreviations were used. In Exeter as elsewhere these included A.R.P. (Air Raid Precautions), A.T.S. (Auxillary Territorial Service), A.F.S. (Auxillary Fire Service), N.A.A.F.I. (Navy, Army and Air Force Institutes), N.A.R.P.A.C. (National Air Raid Precautions Animals Committee), N.F.S. (National Fire Service), W.A.A.F. (Women's Auxiliary Air Force), W.R.N.S. (Women's Royal Naval Service) and W.V.S. (Women's Voluntary Services for Civil Defence).

The 1940s changed Exeter in many ways, some more obvious than others. Queuing came into its own during the second world war and it was said to have been first introduced locally during wartime by bus conductors who gave instructions in South Street on how to form an orderly line. There was a mania for them. In June 1943 one local writer noted:

Queues become more and more sociable, it seems, and quite a lot of people rather like them for their friendly and newsy contacts. They also attract the frankly curious. The other day, for instance, two young fellows lined up with the rest outside the Guildhall and progressed gradually through the entrance and into the main hall without knowing at all why they were there. Arrived almost at the tables, one of them exclaimed: 'Good heavens! It's only rations books!' Goodness knows what they had expected but both beat an immediate retreat.[27]

Many other facets of life changed but are less easy to spot than the great gaps of historical buildings in the city's landscape.

— Part One —

The War Years, September 1939 to August 1945

— Autumn 1939 —

Exeter experienced a sense of anticipation in the first two days of September and then on the 3rd life suddenly altered. It changed and not just for the next six years. Exeter would not be able to return to as it was in early September 1939.

On the 3rd Britain issued an ultimatum to Germany to withdraw from Poland, invaded two days before. Shortly afterwards Britain, France, India, Australia and New Zealand declared war. Within a fortnight German and Russian forces overwhelmed Poland and by the end of the month Germany and the Soviet Union signed a boundary and friendship treaty. A British Expeditionary Force went to France but little happened through the autumn. In October Poland surrendered to Germany, HMS *Royal Oak* was sunk at Scapa Flow and the naval base there was bombed. In November the Luftwaffe dropped magnetic mines in the Thames and several vessels including one from Japan were sunk. In December conscription was extended to all men aged between 19 and 41. The age limit was later

6–7. Two adverts which appeared in the Express & Echo in the first few weeks of the war. The tone quickly changed.

raised to 60 although some key occupations were reserved. One of the most dramatic events happened in South America where the *Graf Spee* was tracked down and engaged in the River Plate. It was subsequently scuttled and HMS *Exeter* dramatically returned, safe but damaged, to Plymouth.

Apparently Exeter was unsurprised by the declaration of war; the mayor noted 'the present crisis has been anticipated, I think, from the day we commenced to re-arm'.[28] On the last day of peace one popular film was *Fire Over England* with Flora Robson but shortly afterwards the cinemas and the Theatre Royal closed. They reopened days later. The city was already receiving hundreds of evacuee children. Crowds gathered in Northernhay to watch them arrive at Central Station. By the 9th some 900 children were billeted, mainly in St Thomas. The first blackout was on the night of the first and in these early weeks a large number of weddings took place. Many grooms were in the armed services. Preparations were made in the cathedral to protect treasures: the ancient glass in the East Window was removed and Bishop Bronscombe's tomb was wrapped in cotton wool and then encased in sand bags.[29] On the 13th Deller's Café opened a recreation

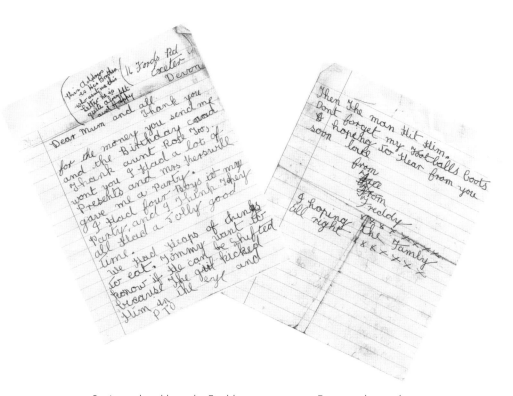

8. An undated letter by Freddy, an evacuee to Exeter, to his mother.

9. Deller's Café, the premier spot in the city.

room for the armed forces in its ballroom.[30] The first casualty of the blackouts happened in the middle of the month: two men fell into the canal and another into the basin. The latter drowned. On the 15th there was a rush on petrol; it was rationed the following day. About then local people were amused to hear newspapers in Adelaide and New York had reported Exeter would be Britain's wartime capital.

Within a fortnight of the arrival of evacuees complaints were lodged about them and attempts made to move them from their hosts. One woman reported her four-year-old evacuee was 'absolutely unmanageable' and another host was allegedly on the verge of a breakdown. The Chief Billeting Officer commented the 'war was getting on everybody's nerves, and that people must realise that it would take some time to become accustomed to having strangers invading the sanctity of their homes'.[31] It was claimed some were 'freezing out' their guests and acting 'selfishly, unpatriotically and very short-sightedly' in wanting only people of their own class and station. In these first few weeks a large number of pets, particularly large dogs, were destroyed. It was thought owners could not afford to feed them. In comparison, in London hundreds of thousands of cats were destroyed by veterinarians merely in the first few days of September.[32] By the 27th between 3,000 and 4,000 articles of clothing were distributed by the Mayoress to needy evacuees. On the 29th some 20,000 Exonians filled in their National Registration Forms. They recorded the names and other particulars of all persons at home that night and this information was used for identity and ration cards. By the end of the month there was public discussion on the cost of civil defence and the local press debated whether more garden allotments were necessary. There were also questions over whether the white stripes, which had been painted on lampposts and walls at street corners to aid night traffic, would continue when war was over.[33]

On 13 April 1939 the town clerk had been appointed A.R.P. Controller and by the 16th of September was regarded by the *Express & Echo* as the personal 'nerve centre' of local civil defence.[34] At the end of September the council met for the first time since war was declared to discuss the work of the Local War Emergency Committee. It had met daily since April. There were rumours throughout Exeter regarding money spent on civil defence. The councillors complained of wild expenditure and of being excluded from decision-making. One man noted views would be different had the city already been bombed. In spite of adverse comments, the council approved the Committee's work.[35]

Preparations continued in October. 'Dig for Victory' was the new motto for gardeners;[36] the city was already looking at the provision for allotments. It was claimed the reception of evacuees was successful except for some expected 'friction and difficulties'. An editorial in the *Express & Echo* questioned whether food supplies would be short; it noted rationing was inevitable during wartime but doubted there would be deprivation. There was an A.R.P. exercise including a simulated mustard gas explosion at Livery Dole. The first air raids in the country were along the Firth of Forth but one city councillor, in a continuing debate on the cost of civil defence, argued for a reduction in staff numbers because Exeter 'was officially regarded as nearly the safest place in England'. There were 2,345 persons in the A.R.P. but all were voluntary except for 214 men and women. One of Exeter's most noteworthy events was the opening of the new cattle market and it was noted there were more horses to be seen in the city than before the start of petrol rationing. Everyday events continued such as going to the cinema: Robert Donat could be seen in *Goodbye Mr Chips* and Cary Grant appeared in *Gunga Din*. One sailor was found drunk at night in Cathedral Close and fined. He had been through the Boer War, the Western Front and the Russian Revolution but when he returned to his hometown he found some kind of 'cross, side-stepping machine' which always landed him in trouble.[37]

In November the Western Front remained quiet and England watched for news of its soldiers. Early in the month there was a slight easing of blackout times. On the 11th there was an unusually poignant remembrance ceremony at the War Memorial in Northernhay. Press censorship became more noticeable with information less available. At the prison there was a continued dispute with prisoners: loud noises were made, particularly at night, disturbed the neighbourhood. One resident likened it to the 'roar of animals' and another thought the language disgusting. One prisoner was said to specialise in making 'too-realistic imitations of the howling of cats' but, most interesting of all, it was claimed prisoners were shouting 'We are Englishman' and 'We want to fight'.

By the 17th the number of official evacuees was 779 and there were a further 933 unofficial evacuees, referred to as refugees, from throughout the country, including as far as Edinburgh, as well as from continental cities such as Vienna and Berlin. The number of midwives was increased from 7 to 9: a great number of expectant mothers had moved to Exeter. On the 22nd a car was stolen whilst its owners were at the Odeon. They had left behind Bill, their blind thirteen-year-old terrier, and he turned up later that night, without the car, after being found eight miles outside Exeter wandering in a confused state. Also that day Vera Brittain, the pacifist and feminist, spoke at an Exeter meeting of the Peace Pledge Union. She implored members not to become 'degenerates' through hating Germans, to view any casualties amongst them with pity and to begin planning for a better world. She stressed that on no account should Germany be bombed and said 'I would rather endure the results of an air raid myself than make the German people suffer'. A week later there was another A.R.P. exercise. It included an incident at Pancras Lane, now within the Guildhall Shopping Centre.[38]

By the beginning of December the Christmas shopping season was busy and exceeded some expectations. Sirens were tested and on the 4th several hundred parents of London evacuees arrived by train for an official visit. One said 'It is one of the hardest things for a mother to give up her kiddies to another woman's care, but after our visit to their foster people I came home feeling quite differently.'[39] The mayor thanked five city officials for their hard work and added 'I am convinced that one of the reasons for our immunity from air attacks up to the present has been the preparedness of our Air Raid Precaution Services which are, I presume, as well known to the enemy as to ourselves'.[40] One male and one female student at the University College of the South West declared themselves Conscientious Objectors and were exempted from military service on condition they remained in teacher training. One was a member of the Church of England and the other a Baptist. A full moon on Christmas night made it possible to walk in safety in Exeter but there were still complaints about prams and dogs on pavements during blackout hours.

One writer in the newspaper reflected 'for years it has been a commonplace that history is in the making. Let us hope that in 1940 such a chapter of history will be written by the Allies, and the freedom-loving peoples, large and small, now outside the conflict, as will make every Briton proud to have lived through the year'.[41]

— 1940 —

JANUARY

A national scrap metal appeal was launched[42] and Exeter gradually contributed considerable amounts of unwanted metal. The decade began with celebrations throughout the city. On New Year's Night at Deller's Café, at the corner of Bedford and High Streets, some 400 guests gathered for a themed evening entitled 'Motoring through the twentieth century'. The menu featured Crème Nuffield [Lord Nuffield was the founder of Morris Motors] followed by fillet of sole Rover or chicken a la Cowley [near Oxford which was the Morris works] with Longbridge sauce [named after the Austin works in Birmingham]. But the tone of the editorial for the first *Express & Echo* of 1940 was more sombre. The editor wished his readers a happy new year, apologised for sounding superficial and wrote 'let us therefore face 1940 not with soothing clichés but with a sense of realities. There is a job to be done, and the sooner it is completed the sooner will the foundations have been laid for that universal happiness which, it is hoped, will be the keynote of the new world that is to be'. A week later rationing began. By the 8th all residents had to register for meat with a butcher and on that day bacon and ham (four ounces), butter (four ounces) and sugar (twelve ounces) were all restricted. One Exeter resident later remembered she started shopping with a mantra of 'bacon, marg., lard, cheese, sugar' to remind herself of what she had to acquire. Food supplies were of general concern and even the City Mental Hospital aimed to be self-supporting: it grew all its own vegetables and a herd of cows supplied enough milk for its needs. The war featured on the front pages of every newspaper and among the stories was the escape of Mrs T. M. Snow, wife of the British Minister to Finland, from Helsinki to Cleve House, the family home.

Life, and death, carried on including the deaths of residents such as Alderman Nethercott, known as the Grand Old Man of Heavitree. He had begun public service in the 1890s and had remarked upon how he had seen his parish change from being 'truly rural to thickly-populated'. One of his stories was that Burnthouse Lane had been given its name because fires were frequent in its farm buildings and sheds. Some public entertainment reflected the war: the pantomime at the Theatre Royal, *Aladdin*, had references to Hitler and at the Savoy Edward G. Robinson appeared in *Confessions of a Nazi Spy*. By coincidence, *Aladdin* was the last pantomime performed during the First World War in Exeter. Escapism could be found later in the month with Bette Davis and Humphry Bogart in *Dark Victory*, Bela Lugosi in *White Zombie* and Ronald Colman in *The Man Who Broke the Bank at Monte Carlo*.[43]

The city had 751 evacuees in its schools and three trains brought 288 family members from London to visit. One parent reportedly said 'We have a lot to be thankful for, and the billeting parents deserve every credit for it. My children are so fat & rosy that at first I did not recognise them'. Mr Percy Ball of Lambeth came to see his younger brother in Buddle Lane. He thought the boy was losing his Cockney accent while other children were said to have acquired Devon accents. Twenty children from Dr Barnardo's homes were lodged at Coaver on Topsham Road.[44]

Even the lives of pets were touched by war preparations. One resident wrote to the *Express & Echo* wanting to exercise his dog in public parks during daylight hours given the difficulties of walking during blackout. There were also worries about possible air attacks and the A.R.P. devised a scheme for first aid squads for animals; the National Air Raid Precautions Animals Committee, known as N.A.R.P.A.C., tried to look after animals hurt through bombing.

The employment of women in jobs previously the preserve of men caused difficulties. At a meeting of the Devon Farmers' Union an official said 'I admire the pluck of the city girls and young women who have given up 'cushy' jobs in the towns and cities and expressed willingness to work as agricultural workers for the duration. It is most patriotic on their part, but I do not want any misapprehensions on the matter. There is a great deal of work on the farm which is not fit for women to do, I am not prejudiced against women doing light work on the farm. The Women's Land Army can be a very useful supplement to our skilled and able-bodied male labour, but cannot be a substitute for it. We must have able-bodied men on the land'.

Reports were made concerning damage made to the ancient door of St Mary Steps Church by an Auxiliary Fireman several months before. He had seen a light in the church at night and mistook it for a fire. He discovered it was a sanctuary lamp only after having forced entry. The police raised concerns of the legality of civilians entering houses at will.[45] A special report was made to the Chief Constable of shelters in main streets: he noted some 7,000 people could be accommodated and wrote all shops had been helpful except Hepworths at 187–8 High Street where the manager had referred his enquiries to the firm's solicitors.[46]

One piece of good war news was the return of *HMS Exeter* from the South Atlantic to Plymouth but there were widespread concerns about events on the continent.

FEBRUARY

Spirits were raised by the rescue of some 300 British seamen imprisoned in the *Altmark*. The vessel was found in a Norwegian fiord. Many had been captured by the *Graf Spee*.[47] Meanwhile Exeter was promoted as 'a haven in which to relax in these strenuous times' and tried to appeal to those unable to have holidays on the continent.[48] But blackouts reminded locals that even Exeter was in danger of bombing. Some residents were fined for not following the law and there were a number of deaths attributed to accidents caused by blackouts. In Exeter alone five people had been killed and 122 injured. Summer time was reintroduced in February and lasted through the war.[49] Staff in eighteen firms rehearsed civil defence: only seven firms had not provided employees with proper training. The authorities were concerned the month before to note which of the 2,207 employees in 26 commercial buildings were trained: in one firm, William Bruford & Son, 53 staff were in the building and 3 were trained in anti-gas procedures, two in first aid and six in fire fighting.[50] Meetings throughout the city reflected aspects of the war including a lecture at St Stephen's Church in which a native of Warsaw reported Jews 'were being slaughtered wholesale for no reason other than that they happened to be Jews'.

Public entertainment included Johnny Weissmuller and Maureen O'Sullivan being featured in *Tarzan Finds A Son* at the Savoy and Spencer Tracey and Mickey Rooney in *Boys' Town* at the Plaza. Later in the month Errol Flynn and Olivia de Havilland were in *Dodge City* and Basil Rathbone starred in *The Hound of the Baskervilles*.[51]

In the middle of the month Miss Beatrix Cresswell died. She was one of Exeter's most respected historians. All through February there was continuing discussions over whether the city should preserve two ancient buildings on West Street. It was noted in the *Express & Echo* 'there was a rich archaeological atmosphere about this particular quarter which deserved much more attention than it has received in the last few decades, and we should not be in a hurry to scrap the remnants.' On the 23rd a local landmark was demolished: the 120 foot high chimney at the brickworks at Clifton Hill was given four charges of gelignite and came tumbling down. It had been erected in 1870 and some 300 million bricks made there. The works closed because of the war.[52]

On the last day of February, Leap Day, 50,000 people cheered 8 officers and 80 men from HMS *Exeter* on their way from St David's Station to the Guildhall. The Freedom of the City was given to the Commanding Officer. In Plymouth, the week before, there had been a public dance where 'the Spee Song' was a feature.[53] The chorus was:

> *If you meet Old Hitler face to face*
> *Just tell him this from me,*
> *That we're the boys who sunk the Spee.*

MARCH

Meat rationing was extended from ham and bacon to other meat: the amount changed but initially everyone over the age of six was allowed 1s 10d per week and smaller children were allowed 11d weekly.[54]

A high rate of illness among the staff of the city's hospital was blamed on the blackouts and the general 'fear of machines in the sky which have been invented by mankind to kill mankind'. It was reported some 3,000 London schoolchildren could be evacuated to Exeter 'if and when' air raids occurred. Meanwhile the council's allotments committee agreed another group of evacuees, blind adults, could have their allotments at Stoke Hill rent-free. Adverts in local papers exhorted farmers to 'Plough Now! By day . . . and night . . . and beat the weather! Farmers! By ploughing now you can win the equivalent of a mighty naval battle! By providing food for the nation and by making your farms self-contained and independent of overseas feeding stuffs, you make both our shipping and our money available for buying munitions from abroad. Win your *Graf Spee* battle of production by ploughing up now!'[55]

APRIL

The War Emergency Committee discussed the provision of public shelters. There was a council debate regarding reducing the annual clothing allowance for the police from one jacket, two new pairs of trousers, one helmet, two pairs of black gloves and one pair of white gloves to one pair

BUYING PERMIT

This permit contains........60........Utility Furniture Units
and the following Priority Dockets

........10........Curtain material

........................Floor covering

........................Mattresses

........................Blankets

........3........Sheets

To be quoted in any correspondence

Reference Number 6822954

The person to whom this permit is issued **MUST** complete these particulars **BEFORE** using it

1. Name ....Mrs. S. W. Pheck,

2. Address ....

3. National Registration (Identity Card) Number or Service Number and Rank ....

AREA OF VALIDITY

For the purpose of obtaining Utility Furniture, this permit may be used only at a shop within a radius of 15 miles of the address to which the furniture is to be delivered or anywhere in.......

Date of issue.......28 JUN 1948

Please see Notes inside the front and back covers

51—3069

10. There was a lack of imported timber early in the war and the sale of furniture became restricted. The government introduced Utility Furniture as a means of making distribution fairer and the scheme continued after the war. This Buying Permit was dated 1948.

of new trousers only for men with over five years' service, no helmets for men with more than three years' service, one pair each of black and white gloves and no jackets for men with over five years' service. The Allotments Committee reported 120 plots had been provided at Stoke Hill and 47 at the Hylton estate. A further 232 plots were being arranged elsewhere including 38 at Marsh Barton on the site of the new abattoir.[56]

Several hundred Civil Servants were living in Exeter. Plans to move from London had been made the previous year. In April the Admiralty informed Exeter's Chief Billeting Officer it was arranging for more staff to be billeted at 19 addresses throughout the city including 9 Bartholomew Terrace, 23 Whiteway Drive, 37 Duckworth Drive, 46 Polsloe Road and 48 West Grove Road.[57] The Mayor wrote an open letter about the disappointing response to other evacuees: he deplored householders who had not offered voluntary accommodation to evacuee children. He also ordered a new survey of potential housing for the 3,000 children expected under the government's evacuation scheme.[58]

11. Members of the National Fire Service.

Mr W. J. G. Bradford, a Conscientious Objector aged 23, was refused employment with the Auxiliary Fire Service. A tribunal stipulated he had to serve in a full-time capacity but local firemen warned they would resign rather than work with him. At this time one other Objector was turned away and another was employed as a hospital orderly.[59]

Even in the midst of the war there was still serious crime: an attempted armed robbery took place at a newspaper and general shop at St David's Hill. A young man approached the cashier and said 'I want a shilling! If it wasn't for creating a scene I'd shoot you'. Fortunately, he was frightened off by a passer-by. Public entertainment included Judy Garland and Mickey Rooney in *Babes in Arms* at the Gaumont.[60]

MAY

On May 10 Winston Churchill became Prime Minister and the Germans invaded France and the Low Countries. Weeks later some 338,000 troops were withdrawn across the Channel from Dunkirk.[61] War preparations continued. The town clerk reported on the cooperation received from private firms regarding civil defence: six had good reports but A. Rice & Company Ltd had failed to reply to requests for information.[62] The council planned 89 public shelters and women were considered as possible conductors for omnibuses. They had to be aged over eighteen and in their first six months of service were to be paid no less than 90 per cent of the wages given to men. It was also announced they would not be employed after the war. Railings were to be removed around the greens in Southernhay and Bedford Circus for scrap iron. It was planned to later take the remaining railings. There was an official drive to make the city more A.R.P.-minded.[63] At the same time the town clerk complained to the Salvation Army of the noise the Army Band made in Goldsmith Street during services: the Control Centre in nearby Waterbeer Street found the music was too loud to hear telephone calls.[64]

An official warning was sent to the council of a risk of enemy parachutists and urged it to find means to make vehicles difficult to obtain; it was suggested owners should remove distributor covers and keys at night to immobilise them. The Police Auxiliary Force also discussed German parachutists. A priority Whitehall telegram was sent to the council: prepare for war refugees from Holland and Belgium.[65]

JUNE

The evacuation from Dunkirk was completed and on the 21st France surrendered to Germany. Suddenly the Germans were much closer and Exeter felt less safe. There were concerns in the council over the use of Countess Wear House by Ashford High School, a private school for girls. A considerable number of voluntary billets were lost in what was already a city crowded with evacuees. The council also protested to London authorities the planned visit of 140 parents of evacuee children would coincide with the arrival of another 675 children. Local resources could not cope with both groups.[66]

Civil defence preparations continued. The number of volunteers for the A.R.P. increased from 41 Wardens to 175, from 15 shelter wardens to 94, from 11 first aid posts to 16, from 3 ambulance drivers and attendants to 5 and from 5 messengers to 21. The number of first aid parties fell from 11 to 10 and there was only one person in 'communications'. The Police Auxiliary Services held an exercise and incidents were staged in each of the wardens' eleven groups. Others had been held in March and May as well as in 1939.[67]

The Dean and Chapter were concerned about potential bombing and made plans for emergency repairs to the cathedral: it was thought that if the flying buttresses were damaged the cathedral builders would not have the resources to make repairs before the entire structure collapsed.[68]

The British Union of Fascists was banned. Various city departments responded to a government request for information regarding possible fascists and communists employed by the council: ten replies were sent informing the government every employee was thought to be loyal to their country. As part of a national roundup, in the beginning of the month action was taken against Italians living locally: six were taken and interned. Also this month the plate glass window of an Italian café in the High Street was smashed in a sign of local feeling.[69]

July

Rationing was extended: two ounces of tea per week were available to each ration book while margarine and cooking fats were put on monthly coupons. There was also an appeal by Lady Reading for aluminium to make airplanes.[70] Seven hundred evacuee children were expected to arrive on the 4th and it was reported to the council that it could expect 2,000 more London evacuees. The Deputy Mayor appealed for billets in St Thomas for 700 children.[71]

This month trenches were dug in open spaces in order to thwart possible landing by the Germans. This included in Countess Wear, Wonford Playing Field, Old Heavitree Sewage Works, Heavitree Pleasure Ground, Hamlin Lane Tip, Cowick Barton Playing Field, Flowerpot Fields and Exwick Fields.[72] There was an A.R.P. Exercise on the 14th in which simulated a midnight attack and a return bombing the following day in which high incendiaries and gas bombs were dropped causing great damage and high casualties.[73]

The city had 38 surface shelters for 1,950 people. Sites included Cathedral Green with 3 shelters for 150 people, Bedford Circus Green with four shelters for 200 people, Exe Island with 2 shelters for 100 people, Belmont Pleasure Ground had a block of 2 for 100 people, St Mary's Green (opposite the Globe Hotel) had one shelter for 50 people as did Mary Arches Street.[74] The lack of toilets in or near shelters was a problem. By the 24th shelters were found with human urine and excrement: the Chief Constable recommended they were locked and only unlocked during an emergency.[75] While a shelter was being built in Bedford Circus Theo Andrews asked for permission to dig a temporary trench, which he called a 'funk hole', opposite his front door. He wrote 'the thunderstorm may easily arrive before the cottage is thatched' and noted at the bottom of the letter 'we are most fortunate that Exeter has not yet been bombed'. Also in July the editor of the *Express & Echo* wrote to the town clerk for clarification of any liability in allowing public use of his building's air raid shelter.[76]

Residents of St Thomas complained to the council that the petrol storage tanks were a target for enemy bombing and needed to be camouflaged. In the following months similar complaints were made regarding Garton & King, the Exeter foundry, and even the Golf & Country Club which had a lightly-coloured frontage. It was suggested the building reflected too much light at night.[77] Over the following weeks King Edward Street and Haven Banks residents requested protection from the potential danger of the tanks. It was even proposed to evacuate the local children. The authorities stressed their best protection was to strengthen the walls of their homes and refused requests to provide water buckets because others would also ask for them.[78]

AUGUST

The war reached the city on the 7th with the first bomb: the *Express & Echo* was able to report only 'five bombs fell on a south west town on Wednesday night, little damage was caused to property, and the only casualties were a middle-aged man who was able to walk to a first aid post, a canary which died from shock and a few chickens'.[79] Mr J. Delaney Little Hatch of Manston Road wrote to the town clerk concerned local people contributed to the bombing. The sirens had sounded at 11.15 at night and he watched the lone plane fly over the city, change course and then repeat its flight over the centre. Other reports confirmed local people left doors and windows open and allowed light to escape. Others had used torches. The chairman of the War Emergency Committee wrote separately that 'without listening to idle chatter or gossip, I have found from responsible persons that in districts as scattered as St Thomas and Burnt House Lane – Newtown & Pennsylvania lights were certainly put on in spite of curtains having been drawn aside in for the night'. Little damage was actually done but, as Mr Little Hatch noted of the pilot, 'an experienced man with a cool head should have bombed the lot'.[80] Six places suffered damage on Charney Avenue, Wardrew Road, the Moreton Inn Court on Cowick Street and Shooting Marsh Stile. The only casualty was at Saville Road while at the Crows Nest on Dunsford Hill a flare merely dropped in the garden.[81]

On the 16th two high incendiary bombs dropped in a field along Bovemoor Lane; the leaded glass of Heavitree Church was shattered and two heifers were killed in a field in Mile Lane.[82] The Police Auxiliary Service was informed 'The Chief Constable will be glad if all concerned will assist in dispelling the foolish rumours which circulated following this raid, which, as showed above, resulted in trivial damage. No other damage has been caused by air raid action in the city during the past 24 hours'.[83] But six days later a telephone was installed at the recently installed public mortuary in Rack Street.[84] The town clerk also made secret arrangements with a Newton Abbot firm for access to a telephone line in case Exeter was bombed and the telephone exchange destroyed. He wanted to maintain communications with the Bristol headquarters of the A.R.P.[85] It was discussed this month whether it was possible to lay seaplane obstructions in the Exe Estuary. Some 4,500 sleepers were needed.[86] The government informed the council of its responsibility for costs of funerals of any enemy airmen. All effects, including clothing and identity discs, had to be preserved and handed over to an RAF officer when asked.[87]

The city recorded the amount of equipment it had received for the 846 Wardens in the A.R.P.: this comprised 930 steel helmets, 1058 c.d. respirators, 564 light oilskin coats, 564 oilskin curtains, 564 oilskin gloves, 705 rubber boots and 643 eye shields.[88] There were also complaints regarding overzealous wardens: in one instance a warden stopped a local woman, Miss R. Packer of Marlborough Road, who was wearing her A. R. P. uniform and carrying identity papers. It was claimed wardens were hindering the war effort.[89]

Near the end of August one resident tried to have the ferry at Haven Banks available at night during air raids and also sought the use of a cellar but both requests were refused.[90] This month the Chairman of London County Council visited Exeter on the 11th to meet evacuee children including a group at St Thomas Play Centre.[91]

September

The Battle of Britain was won and invasion appeared somewhat less likely but the Germans continued to bomb British targets at night. On the 6th a bomb fell through the roof of 48 Normandy Road at 23.30. The front of the house was demolished but the bomb passed through the house and was imbedded in the pavement. Two female residents were unharmed and the bomb was taken to Heavitree Brook where it was later detonated. Some damage was caused to buildings from that explosion.[92] On the 16th at 21.00 two 50 kilo bombs exploded in a field near Cleve House in Exwick but there were no casualties or damage. Bombs fell on the 17th at seven different sites. There was damage but no casualties at Alexandra Terrace, 33 Park Road, 31 St John's Road and Polsloe Road. However, there were three casualties, as well as damage, at 25–8 Blackboy Road and at number 72 there were four dead and the house demolished.[93] A total of 2,584 residents were evacuated and many in Heavitree and Polsloe

12. Blackboy Road, site of the first casualties.

Park districts were not allowed home until unexploded bombs were dealt with; these were found in Park Road and Polsloe Road and detonated at the Barley Lane Quarries. On the 21st, four days after the last bombing, a petition for a shelter was sent from residents of Beaufort Street. They were concerned by the proximity to the railway but the War Emergency Committee decided they were not sufficiently vulnerable. In September city authorities agreed to pay for the funerals of the four victims in the air raids but thought they could later ask the public to contribute to a general fund. This month illustrated instructions were also sent on 'How to detect unexploded bombs'.[94]

The Watch Committee reported they were considering employing women in the police force. The Secretary of State intimated he would allow up to ten per cent of the overall number of workers to be women. It was hoped they could fill clerical positions.[95]

OCTOBER

The council disputed responsibility for billeting with the Admiralty: it refused to arrange accommodation for civil servants. The council was already administering housing for thousands of evacuees and some forty families were arriving daily.[96] Official figures placed the number of child evacuees at 4,323 and of adult evacuees at 1,333. This included 126 people under the Blind Persons Scheme (17 of whom were children). There were also 30 boys at Sandford Hall Hostel, 26 girls at Loma Loma Hostel and 24 infants at Southlands Hostel. Local officials informed the government 'there are a great number of people with children who have not applied for billeting orders but are waiting for an official certificate from their local authority.' Some were in compulsory billets: there were 77 mothers, 85 children of school age and 86 under the age of five in 26 houses in 11 streets across the city.[97]

It was reported children caught in the streets whilst coming home from school during an air raid drill were refused shelter. A scheme was suggested whereby the letter S would be placed in windows to indicate householders would give shelter to strangers. It was also agreed that omnibuses would continue to operate during daylight when warning sirens sounded but that at night, during blackout, they would stop running.[98]

There was concern that Claridge & Sons, electric sawmills at the Basin, was at risk: it was presented as the 'Achilles heel' as it could give access to saboteurs to a sensitive area.[99] Moon & Sons, a piano firm located in the High Street, was concerned at the potential fire risk posed by 'accumulations' piled up in back premises. The firm pointed out to the council that in an ancient city like Exeter, where modernised shop fronts obscured ancient buildings, a great deal of accumulated items could easily catch on fire from incendiary bombs. The staff had recently cleared its yard and the owner observed in his twice-weekly visits to London he had seen what happened with 'Bread Basket Molotov Bombs'. He hoped Exeter would not suffer the same fate.[100]

NOVEMBER

The council attempted to maintain control of its incomers; in one report it claimed there were 6,025 evacuee children officially billeted in Exeter with another 1,000 sent privately to the city.[101] Another estimate put the figure at 8,093 of which 2,900 were unaccompanied children, 529 were children and adults in organised parties and 4,664 unofficial refugees, that is, 'those not sent out in organised parties and which were billeted or accommodated in empty houses'. These figures did not include civil servants and war workers. In spite of these numbers, one official noted, with despair, that he, or she, could not give any firm figures but that there were 'a considerable number of persons on the city'.[102] During the height of the war preparations homeowners inconvenienced by evacuee children sent complaints. Letters were written as early as September 1939. One couple living at 57 Broadway wrote of an eight-year-old boy from Lambeth as being 'hardly their style' but grudgingly admitted he was 'a good little boy' and Mr Comer of 53 Park Road objected on the 3rd of November to the compensation for housing a family. He complained 'a polished mahogany lavatory seat in the bathroom was deliberately scratched with soap by their boy, also a table cloth and bed spread was damaged by strands of thread being drawn from it. These things I overlooked so I should be fair [in asking for more money]. The father admitted that the boy had a mania for soap, and often when we went to the bathroom found lavatory seat, taps and basin covered with soap'. Both parents were blind and the boy was only two years old. Mr Comer's complaints were dismissed.[103]

An article appeared in the *Western Morning News* on the 18th entitled 'Truth About Exeter'. It was a retrospective report on damage caused by bombing written, claimed by the Acting Editor, to counter propaganda there had been great damage and morale was broken: 'it was part of a deliberate effort to put a stop to alarming rumours and false statements. In Exeter's case it was, of course, intended to give the lie to [Lord] Haw Haw.' City officials wrote to the editor and to the Ministry of Information concerned the report, which stressed Exeter had barely been touched, would incite the enemy. Eleven days later the city suffered its worst air raid and further letters were sent pleading that no further propaganda reports were made. There were two bombs. One landed at the rifle range in Ludwell Lane and destroyed a brick-built storehouse but caused no injuries. The second landed in gardens between Cranbrook and Woodstock Roads. There were four deaths (two men aged 42, one boy of 9 and a girl of only 4) and 33 others were injured mostly from these two streets. The bombing happened at 21.20.[104] The mobile first aid unit dealt with two land mines.[105]

The members of the Police Auxiliary were sent a message, marked confidential, regarding German invasion plans: 'there is reason to think that the enemy's intention to attempt an invasion of this country has been postponed, but it is known that he has large forces maintained in readiness at the invasion ports. Hence the need for constant alertness and readiness to deal with any emergency. Should invasion be attempted, by sea-borne or air-borne troops, the enemy would certainly make use of every possible subterfuge. He is known to be in possession of a large number of British uniforms, complete to the last detail, and it is possible that air-borne or other troops may land in such disguises. There may be occasions on which linguistic tests are useful, and the following sentences may provide clues to common German pronunciation of English'. It was suggested such phrases as 'I thought the plough went through the rough earth' would betray the Germans who would pronounce it 'I tort de plow wentt droo de roff ertt'. The suggested sentence 'It was a lucky chance that we were able to land by boat' would have betrayed German origins before the linguistic test was made but most improbable of all to fit into a conversation was 'A Chinese man does not eat jam from jars' ('A Shinees menn duss nott eatt tscham from tschars').[106]

A list was made of nineteen men who had initially volunteered for the City Decontamination Squads and Rescue Parties but who had registered for service in the armed forces. Of these men there were 3 tipmen, 2 sweepers, 2 dustmen, 6 lorry drivers, 3 labourers, 1 mason, 1 charge hand and 1 motor mechanic. The government enquired into the number of employees at the city's major firms. It was reported that Willey & Co. had 1,100, Colson & Co. 290, Walton & Co. 200, Bobby & Co. 183, J. Wippell & Co. (at Buller Road) 150, Exeter Laundries 150 and Western National Omnibus Co. 138.[107]

The council discussed a proposal to open cinemas on Sundays between five and ten-thirty at night. The Mayor cast the deciding vote in favour. Christmas treats were arranged for evacuee children: the Education Director of Plymouth sent £1 4s for the 24 Plymouth children in Exeter and London County Council sent £10 10s. The intention was to keep children from evacuation areas during Christmas.[108]

December

Bristol was heavily bombed, following which school children were sent to Exeter. The City of London was badly bombed late in December. In Exeter two Auxiliary Firemen were found drunk and absent from their stations on Christmas Eve and suspended. It was pointed out that no Public Air Raid Warning would have been possible. A report was made into establishing underground first aid posts. Seven places were investigated (the Arcade cellars, Carr & Quick's beneath Civic Hall, a cellar at 59 Magdalen Street, Exeter Dispensary semi-basement, Quay cellars, Rougemont Hotel Lower Ballroom semi-basement).[109]

The City Librarian informed the council he had moved the city's ancient manuscripts from the library's muniments room but was concerned by arrangements for the Control Centre situated in their place. He wanted the issue of the evacuation of the library clarified: were the public to continue to shelter beneath the stairs or were they to be told to go to Bedford Circus where the nearest public shelter was located?[110]

The Minister of Transport sent a message to members of the Police Auxiliary: he wrote 'road accidents are up. Numbers of cars on roads down. Something very wrong here. Black-out, I know, makes driving difficult. Pedestrians are invisible, and yet think they are not. I have seen some very bad driving just when the first warning sounds at night. I know one wants to get home quickly, more so does someone on foot. Be doubly careful under these conditions. Remember this all the time. You are like a soldier in a tank, protected from damage in a collision. The pedestrian is not. What may only be a bent wing for you, may mean hospital for life to the citizen you hit. The danger from the air is quite enough at present. See to it there is very little from the ground'.[111]

The town clerk wrote to the editor of the *Western Morning News* regarding a news report. The paper had reported the city authorities were not keen for local inhabitants to use sand to put out bombs. It was, according to the clerk, 'a mischievous attempt to cause public alarm'. A secret report was sent to the town clerk regarding unexploded parachute mines or bombs. It was stressed the 'enemy has shown himself singularly quick to adapt his methods to our tactics. The fact we have knowledge of the existence of booby-traps and other devices must not be disclosed.'[112]

— 1941 —

JANUARY

The new year began with mixed feelings about the course of the war. The *Express & Echo* wished its readers 'Good fortune keep you company, and may you, in the year to be, see Victory, Peace, Felicity'. The vicar of St Mark's Church remarked to his congregation 'I am sure when historians come to record the reactions of the people of this country to the deadly attacks of the enemy their record will be that, in the annals of English history, never have English men, women and children displayed greater bravery, courage and endurance.'[113] But in the closing days of December London had been badly bombed and in January Amy Johnson was lost, and British bases on Malta were bombed.

Christmas parties were held for children at Welfare Centres including at St James' Institute and Southernhay Methodist Hall. In the midst of the seasonal festivities war preparations continued. The Chief Constable installed himself in the former rooms of the A.R.P. Control Centre in

Waterbeer Street. He was concerned whether the building could withstand a direct hit.[114] Fire prevention was a matter of great concern: the Chamber of Trade started a campaign to increase the number of Fire Bomb Squads and sent 1,500 appeals. Meanwhile, cathedral authorities were looking for 50 fire-watchers. Bags of sand were distributed throughout the city. This month the fire-watching scheme was introduced whereby men between the ages of sixteen and sixty were liable to serve.[115] The Salvation Army raised £400 for a mobile canteen which was to be used for troops and the civilian population if needed.[116] Dr John Caldwell of the University College of the South West spoke at the Guildhall on allotments as part of the national 'Grow More Food' campaign. Uniforms were being organised for the Auxiliary Fire Service. Firms in Dundee, Norwich, Bradford, Gateshead, Edinburgh and Luton were successful unlike any local company. The council ordered 100 single-breasted tunics, 125 pairs of trousers, 100 caps, 100 rubber water-proof coats and 150 blue dungaree training overalls.[117]

Efforts continued to be made to keep everyone falling into line in the war effort. Six residents were fined for blackout offences, three of them paid a fine of one pound, and one man, Wilfred Dymond of 19 Duckworth Road, was fined ten shillings for having an unauthorised bicycle lamp.[118] A resident of Magdalen Street tried to circumvent rationing by importing butter from County Cork. After being caught and fined one pound she claimed she had felt unwell and thought butter would improve her health. A fire-watcher, who lived in Brewery Place, was told by the judge his stealing £2 10s 9d and a pair of spectacles whilst working was 'damnable' and 'just as bad as a case of looting'. Further order was achieved when queuing was adopted at bus stops. South Street was first and the practice quickly spread to High Street. It was claimed 'order was produced out of chaos' and only a few sharp words by conductors were needed to keep everyone in line.[119]

On the 16th four small high incendiary bombs were dropped but there was slight damage and few injuries; three landed in Fairpark Gardens in Pavilion Place and the other in Magdalen Road some twenty yards from the junction of Fairpark Road. It may have been this attack that the *Express & Echo* reported the following day. It noted there was minor damage from a raid 'in a south west town last night'.[120]

FEBRUARY

Overseas the British raided Tripoli while in Exeter war work included teachers arranging fire-watching in elementary schools and fifty-four allotment plots were provided at Cowick Barton Playing Fields. Another eighteen were added a few months later.[121] The ancient wooden figures around the clock at St Mary Steps Church were removed for safety. The portraits of Princess Henrietta Anne and General Monck in the Guildhall and the civic regalia had already been moved. On the 15th Exeter War Weapons Week began with a procession and exceeded the goal of raising £500,000. The motto was 'England Expects Extra From Exeter'.[122] The Police Auxiliary Force was told, in a confidential circular, circular boards found at night with lights could explode thirty minutes after landing. There were two types of German parachute mines: both were cylindrical, 2 ft 6 inches in diameter and the parachute was made of mixed green and white artificial silk. Public entertainment included Errol Flynn in *The Sea Hawk* and Charlie Chaplin in *The Great Dictator*.[123]

After the bombing of Bristol its Chief Education Officer was informed by his Exeter counterpart:

I think it is advisable to let you know what the real position is in Exeter at the present time so far as educational facilities are concerned – this in order that your committee and teachers will not be disappointed and expect something which it is quite impossible for us to give you, even with the best will in the world.

First and foremost, our city is severely overcrowded – our peacetime population of 67,000 is now not far short of 100,000. The number of official and unofficial evacuees from London, Kent, Croydon, Penge and 23 other Local Education Authorities at present is only just below our own native scholar population. Every school in Exeter is carrying nearly double its peace-time roll. Gymnasiums, assembly halls, staff-rooms, craft-rooms, laboratories, etc. are all used for classroom purposes and every available private Hall in the City has been taken and occupied. There is not another Hall or square inch of accommodation left in Exeter unless we start utilising churches.

The question of billets is one for the Exeter Billeting Authority but I am informed that your children will necessarily be billeted all over the City – just where billets are available. There can be no question of 'identity' of Bristol schools. Your scholars will have to be 'merged' into the local schools – a policy which was forced upon us (and most other reception areas) last June owing to increased numbers.

Furthermore, I am just afraid that our existing full-time system of education will now break down under the strain of additional numbers and that it may be necessary for certain schools to go on the 'double-shift' system when your parties arrive – most undesirable but there we are. So far we have endeavoured to get 'a quart into a pint pot' but to put more is impossible.

We shall look after your children and make them comfortable and happy but I do want you to get a true picture of the educational problem with which we are faced.[124]

13. A Home Guard exercise at an unknown location.

It was estimated that by the end of the month there were 12,600 official evacuees with possibly the same number of those who had moved privately. There were also 7,000 Bristol schoolchildren who had recently arrived.[125]

MARCH

British forces overwhelmed the Italian fleet off Greece and rationing hit further when jam, marmalade and syrup were put on monthly coupons.[126] In Exeter plans were made to erect a rifle position within the shrubbery at the junction of Barrack and Wonford Roads. There was dismay amongst local officials that the Home Guard discontinued fire-watching and fire-fighting.[127] The Chief Constable was not happy with wardens issuing traffic instructions during air raid warnings; he pointed to an accident caused by the 'ill-considered actions of a warden suddenly calling on the driver of one motorcar to stop'. This might have been the incident at 22.20 on the 5th at the Exmouth junction of the Southern Railway in which an enemy plane machine-gunned the area but in itself caused no damage or injuries.[128]

A regional official came to discuss plans for a possible fall of large quantities of unexploded para-mines.[129] There was an official notice from Whitehall of the imminent delivery of indoor shelters by the end of the month. These became known as Morrison Shelters, named after the Home

Secretary, Herbert Morrison. By the end of the war over a million were in use throughout the country. The aim was to provide indoor shelters because many people no longer left their beds during air raid warnings for Anderson or public shelters.[130] Public shelter rules were impressed upon the defence authorities. These included that no person should:

> be drunk, offensively unclean or verminous,
> spit or soil any part of the shelter,
> take into the shelter any loaded firearm,
> leave litter,
> smoke, sing or play any musical instrument,
> beg or collect money,
> sell any article,
> take any dangerous or offensive article.[131]

City officials surveyed firms for the provision of coffin boards and burials in the event of heavy bombing casualties. It was reported one Bedford lorry could accommodate five bodies, there were only seven hearses in the city, that provision had been made to purchase material for 350 canvas shrouds and grave space was allocated for mass burials at High Cemetery and at Exwick.[132]

APRIL

The Germans captured Athens. In Exeter supplies of food remained a high priority. The local waste of food was called scandalous: at a meeting of the Exeter Food Control Committee one half of a two-pound loaf of bread was presented. It had been found that day in the street.[133] The Princess Elizabeth Orthopaedic Hospital reported it was cultivating land at the junction of Barrack Road and Wonford Road for its own use. There was also a meeting at the Guildhall for the managements of all local catering establishments regarding plans to feed the city's residents in emergencies.[134] The menu of meals served at the Civic Hall Centre included cottage pie, mashed carrots and baked bread pudding; rissoles, steamed or mashed potatoes, cauliflower, cabbage, carrots or kale and rice or steamed pudding; meat and potato pie with jam tart or rice pudding; shepherd's pie, cabbage and steamed pudding made of figs, dates or syrup; meat stew, mashed Swedes and apple and custard; vegetable hot pot and steamed pudding; sausages and mashed potatoes with rice pudding; fried fish, mashed potatoes and butter beans, fruit and custard or steamed pudding.[135]

On the 20th a large-scale exercise was held of the civil defence services.

14. Scraps were sought for pigs.

An assessment concluded it would be difficult to house the thousands of refugees expected from a severe bombing. Many houses were already overcrowded and, it was claimed, some were not hygienic. There was also

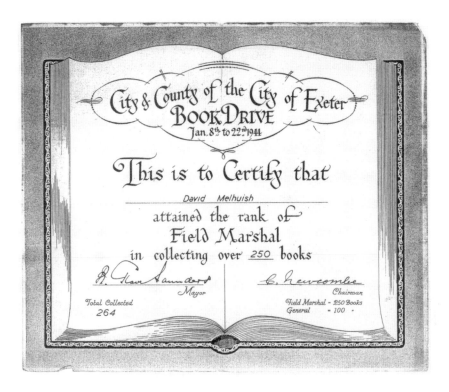

City & County of the City of Exeter
BOOK DRIVE
Jan. 8th to 22nd 1944

This is to Certify that

David   Melhuish

attained the rank of
Field Marshal
in collecting over 250 books

Mayor

Chairman

Total Collected
264

Field Marshal - 250 Books
General   - 100 -

15. Another drive was for scrap paper. Exeter children had a competition to bring in unwanted books and ranks were later awarded based on the quantity found.

a problem with compulsory billeting; there was an 'evasion of duty of some of the householders of the larger houses by *freezing out* so that evacuees will not stay put. News of this has a nasty habit of circulating with the rapidity of an epidemic and evacuees refuse to be billeted at such addresses, generally the evacuees fight shy of all compulsory billets, changing or returning to their homes at the first opportunity'.[136]

The number of refugees was increased by one Belgian, old bones were discovered in the green at Bedford Circus during excavation work, a meeting of the Exeter branch of the Devon & Cornwall Architectural Society appealed for the saving of drawings, photographs and details of old buildings, and the city authorities listed several hundred employees for identity discs.[137]

MAY

British forces withdrew from Greece for Crete but were then driven from that island. HMS *Hood* was sunk off Greenland with the loss of all 1,421 men except three. Rationing was extended to cheese: one ounce per week was allowed although this later was extended to two ounces.[138] In Exeter efforts to increase food production continued. There were discussions regarding a field adjoining Lopes Hall within the Pennsylvania campus of the University College of the South West. The land was being used to graze ponies but it was decided to use it for allotments. The Devon War Agricultural Committee asked the council to set up Pig Clubs in Exeter. It was hoped local people would raise pigs on their allotments.[139] The council were informed 100 local firemen were to be allowed 24 shillings worth of meat per week.[140]

Fire-watchers asked for bags of sand, or just the bags themselves, to fight fires. Local authorities informed them they could not have steel helmets until the government provided them. Similar requests had been made over the last few months.[141]

The town clerk received an official letter which stressed 'I know you have all had a very heavy burden, and although up to the present you have escaped any really heavy bombing, the results of the bombing must have pressed very hardly on you indeed'.[142] Another message was sent warning local authorities the enemy was 'dropping a new type of mine which acts also as a bomb'. There were also new instructions on how to dispose of unexploded gas mines.[143] On the 5th, at 00.23, three high incendiary bombs fell in St Thomas and created two craters in fields and another between the main up and down Exeter to Plymouth GWR line opposite Lynwood Avenue. More than thirty houses were damaged but there were no casualties. Neighbours accommodated the homeless. The following day eight high incendiary bombs left craters in Hill Barton Road and Ringwell Avenue. There was damage but no casualties.[144]

Petitions were sent from residents of Rifford Road asking for the street's white concrete to be tarred over to make it less of a target for enemy planes. Similar petitions were received from residents of Whipton Lane, Vaughan Road and Sweetbrier Lane.[145] Another petition was sent on the 9th by more than 250 residents of 192 households in and around Bartholomew Street regarding Father Browne, a former air raid warden who resided at 8 Bartholomew Terrace. They implored the Chief Constable and the War Emergency Committee to reinstate him because of his qualities (he knew the residents intimately and was thorough in his duty) and the urgency in having no other air raid warden. There is no indication why Browne was released or the outcome other than a later note by the town clerk in support of the Chief Constable's actions.[146]

Local authorities tried to cope with the large number of self-evacuees; the council sought an additional 500 camp beds and 2,000 blankets to

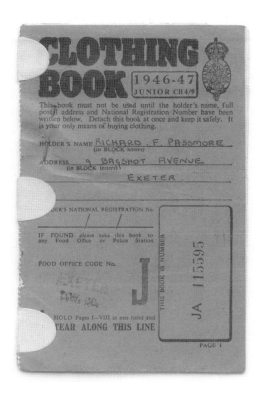

16. *Clothing ration book of Richard Passmore, 1946/7.*

cope with the influx. This month the city sent 3½ tons of clothing to Plymouth which had suffered greatly from bombing.[147]

JUNE

Germany attacked Russia and the course of the war dramatically changed. In Britain clothing rationing was introduced: they were available through coupons on a points system. The system gradually evolved as rationing of food had.

In Exeter the town clerk took exception to an official visit. He wrote to Captain Kitchen of the Air Raid Precautions Regional office at Bristol:

Is it really necessary for one of your regional officers, Captain Driffield Whiting, accompanied by bulldog, to call at my Control Centre at 01.18 hours, on an evening when no alert had been sounded and the staff were resting to be provided with a cup of tea, and then to proceed to inspect two Rescue Party Depots where again the staff were supposed to be resting in the absence of an alert, and without being accompanied by the City Surveyor or his representative on duty? I have not the least objection to a surprise visit at any time, but I do feel, and the City Surveyor feels very strongly, that any such visit should be made in the company of the responsible officer or his representative, otherwise it savours of the kind of 'snooping' which most Britishers heartily dislike . . .

The next day Captain Kitchen apologised but added:

I quite agree that a bulldog, which may be accepted in this office as an honorary regional officer, may not be so accepted by a local authority.[148]

Another complaint was made, this time of the behaviour of two Air Raid Wardens who lived in Oxford Street in St Thomas. One was described as having 'an aggressive bullying nature' who had used bad language with the second, a plumber, who was 'presumably not highly educated, is not as tactful as he might be' but who was able to stand up for himself. The first individual was sent to another part of the city to work as a fire-watcher.[149]

It was observed in the *Express & Echo* that grass was being cut for hay in Dix's Field, the first time for over a hundred years.[150] The daily police report for 26 June recorded concerns over the theft of garden produce from the allotments at Salmon Pool Lane. There were also complaints of the trainees at St Loyes who gathered at the junction of Topsham Road and Burnthouse Lane. The Acting Chief Constable wrote to Dame Buller to stop the annoyance but there was a helpful note in the report that 'it should be remembered that persons suffering from chronic diseases and deformities are often irritable and short-tempered and tact should be used in dealing with them.'[151]

The town clerk was warned by the government that 'the present lull in the German air activity against this country may be of longer or shorter duration. Prophecy is of little value, but what is certain is that while we hope for the best, we must prepare for the worst, and that is a continuation of blitzes of an even more severe character than those we have come through during the autumn and winter months.'[152] Even so, on the 17th five bombs were dropped on Wonford and there were four casualties.[153]

Public entertainment included *Comrade X* with Clark Gable and Penny Singleton in *Blondie Meets The Boss*.[154]

JULY

A meeting coordinated transport priorities in the event of attacks because

Exeter was now seen as a 'target town'.[155] On the 15th a tear gas exercise was held. One on the 9th of May had windy conditions and an early warning had limited its effectiveness. It was announced an exercise would take place and at four o'clock gas was simultaneously released on the High Street in still weather conditions. Wardens used rattles to sound the alarm in the crowded street. The Chief Constable reported 'the effect was magical; people scattered in all directions at once; many disappeared into shops while others moved off down side streets away from the danger area; so quickly did this take place that within half a minute of the first warning sound being heard on the street it was cleared except for those who were wearing respirators. There was no sign of panic whatever, and the police and wardens had no difficulty in carrying out their duties. Shopkeepers responded splendidly, & obeyed without question instructions issued to them about closing doors and windows'. However, he noticed few people carried gas masks and bus drivers operated without respirators. He observed 'children showed no fear and many of them obviously enjoyed passing through the several clouds of gas. The concentration of gas was so good, that, unlike the previous exercise, the public were physically incapable of passing through the area without a respirator. It was attempted by one or two youths on cycles, but they very quickly dismounted and retired out of the area! Twelve people in all were treated at one or another of the first aid posts. One (a member of the RAF), who had his respirator with him, was accompanied by his young lady; she had no respirator, and he decided to suffer with her; both required treatment!'[156]

Students from six schools (including Bishop Blackall, Maynard, Hele's, Mount Radford and Exeter) became part of the enquiry service. Messages were to be sent to each school after a severe attack and transmitted by students after being scrutinized by the master or mistress. Messages were standardized, one being 'In reply to your enquiry, I deeply regret to have to inform you the Casualty Lists show that [blank] was killed by enemy action on [blank].[157]

It was reported to the council's Allotment Committee that the Stoke Hill and St Leonards Allotment Association decided against raising pigs but the association for St Thomas was still considering the idea.[158]

AUGUST

The Atlantic Charter was signed by President Roosevelt and Prime Minister Churchill: it jointly declared the peace aims of the two governments.

A meeting was held at the Guildhall with regional food officers. The

Divisional Food Officer explained 'we want to make plans as far as we can in advance to meet the difficult situations which might occur from enemy action in one form or another. Invasion is very much in the air'. He informed them food stores would last a minimum of fourteen days. Two posters, which featured German parachutists, soldiers and sailors, were posted but government instructions stipulated they were to be situated inside certain buildings and not in view of the general public.[159] At the beginning of the month there were concerns raised on the amount of flammable materials being stored on timber premises at Exe Island; wooden sheds there were full of waste rags. There was slight damage after a bombing incident at Anthony Road.[160] Finally, an assessment was made of the capacity for corpses at the temporary mortuaries: 138 at the Rack Street Schools site, 30 at Whipton Institute and 25 at the Countess Wear village hall.[161]

September

By the first of the month ninety-three buildings were requisitioned, including 4 Albert Street, 2 & 13 Bartholomew Street, 100 Monks Road, 15 Magdalen Road and 10 Salutary Mount. A 'Help Your Neighbour' Scheme was introduced: residents were asked to arrange with a neighbour at least half a mile away to live with them if their homes were bombed. All unnecessary iron and steel railings were to be requisitioned for scrap. Householders could claim exception if railings were of special artistic merit or of historic interest.[162] It was reported to the council that 648 allotment plots of nearly 43 acres was recently utilised together with just over 100 acres of 1,350 existing permanent plots. The city also had 400 privately-owned allotment plots.[163] A report was made of the number of cleared lofts: the government had issued an order that unnecessary items were to be removed in order to make the city less of a fire hazard in the event of possible bombings. Some 152 roads had been finished with the lofts of 6,586 houses cleared.[164]

October

Another meeting of the region's food officers was held. The town clerk was concerned about maintaining sufficient supplies of food if there was an invasion. He said 'When Exeter is completely cut off I must know where I stand. All food would be requisitioned immediately.' He was told to close all city shops and take control of stocks but had continuing worries about supplying food to an estimated 30,000 troops in the surrounding area.

The government agent informed him the military would make their own arrangements.[165]

The city librarian wrote to the town clerk regarding arrangements for running of the Control Centre. It had been removed from Waterbeer Street to the library's basement. He was concerned building would flood from any water thrown by the fire services. The clerk responded there was not a problem but the librarian wrote again insisting he had greater personal knowledge.[166] There were also problems at nearby Rougemont House where the Control Centre staff lodged: traps were needed for the mice inhabiting their bedrooms[167] but it was three years later, in January 1945, that the council was able to claim a general campaign to destroy vermin succeeded. The Control Centre staff was told their telephone line had been tapped and that conversations noted regarding air raid damage with colleagues who were off duty. Authorities were taking a serious view of it.[168]

Four incendiary bomb huts were to be built at Heavitree Pleasure Ground, St Thomas Pleasure Ground, Wonford Playing Fields and the Green in Old Tiverton Road. The council arranged to purchase sixty sets of elm coffin boards for possible heavy casualties arising from bombing.[169]

November

The number of evacuee children from London was given at 2,548, with 2,084 of them over the age of five.[170] There were continued concerns over evacuees having bugs. Some bedding given by the council was returned infected. There were 317 waterproof sheets loaned, 254 mattresses, 1,209 beds, 7,564 blankets and 2 sheets.[171] On the 19th the Exeter Soup Kitchen was wound up after 72 years of operating for the poor.[172] A Dispatch Rider Letter Service was in operation for defence purposes. On its south-east run it left at 10.30 am daily and after running to the RAF base at the airport the rider went to Broadclyst, Honiton, Colyton, Sidmouth and Lympstone before returning.[173]

Concerns were raised over an incident at St Germans House in Pennsylvania at the end of October. A report was sent by the Emergency Feeding Officer that:

on Saturday last (25th October), Miss Rowe of the W.V.S. accompanied by an officer of the Home Guard (Captain Bullard) called at St German's Reinforcement Depot at 6.30 pm. Captain Bullard stated to Leading Fireman Mallock, one of the residents at the Depot, that he had come to commandeer a room at St German's for thirty men of the Home Guard from 10 o'clock that night until 3.30 on Sunday morning and that they must be provided with hot beverages and cakes. Fireman Mallock suggested that Captain Bullard and Miss Rowe should see Mrs Odell, the resident cook, but Miss Rowe declined and asked that a telephone call should be made to Fire Brigade Headquarters. Fireman Mallock replied that the Fire Brigade had no jurisdiction in anything connected with St German's Depot and then Miss Rowe decided to telephone Miss Adam (Supervisor of the Education Committee's School Canteens) at her home address. This Miss Rowe did, stating, 'I wish to introduce Captain Bullard of the Home Guard'. Captain Bullard then repeated to Miss Adam what he had previously stated to Fireman Mallock, viz., that he was commandeering a room at St German's and that hot beverages and cake must be supplied to the 30 men. Miss Adam replied that she had no power to give permission for the Home Guard to enter St German's and that she would get in touch with Mr Downe, officer-in-charge of Reinforcement Depots, who was at Staplake Mount Depot. To this Captain Bullard replied that this was not necessary as he had authority to take premises anywhere at any time for the Home Guard and that he was not 'carrying on and issuing his instructions' and that Lieut. Ball and 30 men of the Home Guard would arrive at 10 pm. As Mrs Odell (age 62) was the only resident cook at St German's Depot, Miss Adam went to St German's, arriving about 7.45 pm. Lieut. Ball and the 30 men of the Home Guard arrived at 10 pm, walking through the back entrance and took possession of the Mess Room. They entirely ignored Miss Adam and Mrs Odell but when, towards 10.30 pm, Miss Adam asked Lieut. Ball how long they proposed to stay on the premises, the reply was 'until the end of the exercise at 3.30 am'. He asked for hot cocoa and slab cake to be provided at once. This was done. When asked if the staff must wait up until 3.30 am, his reply was 'Most certainly'. As Miss Adams had her aged mother with her, they returned home at 11.50 pm, but Mrs Odell (aged 62) was unable to go to bed until 3.50 am, twenty minutes after the Home Guard had departed. Note: 10 shillings of cocoa and cake was provided and the telephone was used on five occasions. The Mess Room was left in a filthy condition'.[174]

December

The second sudden change in the war occurred when the United States declared war on Japan on the 7th following the attack on the naval base at Pearl Harbour in Hawaii. Among the men killed was Charles Lawrence, the only son of an emigrant from Exeter to the United States.[175] Germany and Italy declared war on the United States and Hong Kong surrendered

"MOTHER!!"

"They're coming Ethel! Show a bit more leg!"

17-21. First in a series of cartoons by George Stillings, known as Stil, 1946. They were drawn in Exeter but are representative of American servicemen in cities, towns and villages across England.

"ONE YANK AND THEY'RE OFF !"

"...AND PLEASE SAVE ME AN AMERICAN !".

"DON'T DESPAIR. GERTRUDE ! I HEAR THERE'S ANOTHER THOUSAND COMING IN NEXT WEEK".

to Japan. Food rationing changed with the introduction of the points rationing scheme. Items of food which had disappeared from shops were reintroduced, each item was given a number of points and ration book holders were allowed initially sixteen points a week. At first canned meat, fish and vegetables were placed on points and other commodities were later added.[176]

The University College of the South West refused a request to use a field near Lopes Hall for allotments because it was used for sport by 220 female students.[177] The city's war effort was helped by the gift of a mobile trailer kitchen from the Canadian people.[178] The town clerk received a letter from the Ministry of Health questioning the recent decision of the Emergency Committee not to stock water in public shelters. He was told 'I wonder if they know and have considered that Exeter is regarded by the military as a place which may have to be defended against invasion which means of course, that there may be very intensive bombing both by day and by night, with perhaps a large number of people in shelter for very long periods'.[179]

The pantomime at the Theatre Royal was 'Dick Whittington and His Cat'. A Christmas meal was provided for the fire-fighters at St German's House. The menu for dinner was:

Christmas Goose
Apple sauce and stuffing
Roast potatoes
Brussels sprouts

—

Christmas Pudding
Custard sauce

—

Mince pies

—

Cheese and celery

—

Tea

—

Cigarettes[180]

— 1942 —

JANUARY

The city's sheriff commented 'the outstanding feature of 1941 has been the complete unity of all classes in their determination to win through to victory, whatever the cost, and the optimistic spirit and courage with which they had faced disappointments and reverses'.[181]

In Exeter there was a concerted effort to make camouflets better known within civil defence services: these were 'the subterranean cavity formed by the explosion of the bomb and filled with the gas caused by the explosion – carbon monoxide'. They were 'formed when a bomb explodes beneath the surface of the earth and the force of the explosion is insufficient to displace and disperse the soil above the bomb'. Another civil defence exercise was held, this one focused on communications, and the scenario was that the enemy had successfully landed in southern Ireland from which it was bombing the South West.[182]

There was concern from the regional office in Bristol that Exeter's citizens were not taking the threat to their city seriously. The town clerk was told it was a Category A Nodal Point town 'highly likely to be the scene of military operations in the event of invasion'. However, he informed Bristol shortly afterwards he was unable to satisfy local demand for Morrison shelters. He had 600 more applicants than shelters.[183] The City Architect estimated his department would need, for building purposes, 304,000 common bricks, lower than the 324,000 for December but more than the 48,000 in November.[184]

FEBRUARY

It was reported 65 acres had been cultivated for war use including on Southernhay Green, Belmont Pleasure Ground, Flowerpot Playing Fields, Wonford Playing Fields, Belle Island, Bury Meadow Pleasure Ground, Heavitree Pleasure Ground, Cowick Barton Playing Fields, Trew's Weir and Tollard's Farm. In the previous year there were grown 33½ tons of potatoes, 23 cwts of turnips, 2½ cwts of French beans, 235 tons of tomatoes, 92 lbs of peas and 37 marrows.[185]

Housing was tight. One example of this was when 150 women students at the University College of the South West were informed they might have to vacate their lodgings in three halls of residence if required for official purposes.[186]

On the 15th the city experienced another civil defence exercise. The intention was to make locals 'more war-minded'. It began at 10.25 am but there was widespread criticism particularly of the casualty and rescue services who were late or did not show up. Volunteers acted the roles of victims of air attacks and some, such at those at the Clock Tower, were lying on pavements for an hour and a half in severe weather. Wardens suggested the exercise did more harm than good and rescue squad leaders were reported as saying 'considerable harm was done to their keenness and enthusiasm'. The casualty services also thought the exercise failed and blamed it on a breakdown in the message system at control headquarters.[187]

March

War preparations included the arrival of a second batch of twenty communal shelters which cost the city £5,660. Each of them were for 48 persons and sites included Beacon Avenue, Clifton Street and Maple Road. Also, the council expressed its sympathy to the relatives of the crew of HMS *Exeter*[188] and a defensive wire against the enemy was erected near the Cowley Bridge Inn. The National Emergency Washing Service planned three days in the city, at Buddle Lane, Chestnut Avenue and Widgery Road, to provide 'a free service for those people who are unable to wash clothes at home owing to enemy raids'.[189] A conference was held at the University College of the South West with the theme 'Civilian Morale'. Public entertainment included Gary Cooper in *The Westerner*, Lucille Ball in *The Navy Steps Out* and Clark Gable and Rosalind Russell in *They Met in Bombay*.[190]

April

The National Association of Funeral Directors requested the council to discontinue Sunday burials. The council agreed. A meeting of the region's food officers were told 'if communications with Bristol were broken, Cornwall and Devon must be able to function either as counties or, if necessary, as smaller independent units'.[191]

The city suffered the most destruction yet when attacked by the Luftwaffe on the nights of the 23rd, 24th and 25th.[192] The police reported that on the 23rd four people died, on the 24th at least 41 died and another 73 died on the 25th. Destruction occurred throughout the city.[193] Mr S. J. Willey of the National Fire Service, stationed at the divisional headquarters at Crossmead on Dunsford Hill, wrote two reports. In his second, dated the 28th, he noted:

I made a very thorough search of the bombed areas in the hope of finding an incendiary bomb intact and only succeeded in locating two, although as previously stated in my earlier report I found as many as 27 had dropped on one building.

I have dismantled these two bombs and upon investigation found that a slight variation in the construction of the bomb, compared with those that have previously been used inasmuch as a small explosive charge is contained in the small disc at the base of the bomb, situate in such a position as to retain the thermite, but in close proximity to the main charge, which is exploded by the centre pin upon impact.

After dismantling the bomb I carefully removed the disc and made several discs, first of all I dropped it from various heights, and then by sharp blows from the hammer, as it failed to produce any results, I then placed the small disc in a spot of ignited petrol with the result that within a few seconds an explosion took place.

I would suggest that although the explosion would not seem so forceful as that found in the earlier type of incendiary bomb it appears to have the power to spread the thermite, and also the base of the bomb to such an extent as to allow the bomb to become thoroughly ignited.

I would suggest that however small the firing effect may be any doubt as to whether there is sufficient heat in the initial charge to ignite the bomb is instantly overcome, when the heat reaches the second explosive charge.

In conclusion, may I add that Mr McCullock of Princess Risborough attached to Regional Headquarters is now in Exeter, and I have passed on my observations to him, he expressed the remark that my observations were entirely new to him. I told him that I would be submitting my report to the Fire Force Commander, which in due course would no doubt reach his department . . .[194]

Another report was later written of the effectiveness of Morrison shelters. It noted three examples for the April attacks. The first happened in a house in Wonford Street in which a high incendiary bomb exploded 15 feet from the shelter and left a crater some 43 feet in diameter and 15 feet deep. The house was totally destroyed but the two people in the shelter, which was on ground level, were dug out of the rubble uninjured. The shelter was also undamaged. The second incident which was highlighted concerned another house in the same street. This was a cob and brick building and it too was completely destroyed by a direct hit. The bomb hit five feet from the shelter and left a similar crater. Five people were dug out, uninjured, but the state of the shelter was unknown as it remained partially covered by rubble. The third example was of a house in Regent's Park completely destroyed also by a high incendiary bomb; it hit some thirty feet from the shelter and left a crater 48 feet in diameter and 15 feet deep. The shelter apparently did not move and the five occupants were unharmed.[195]

A few days after the attack the commanding officer of C. Platoon 77 Division of the U.S. Army wrote to the town clerk asking for permission to move his vehicles from West Avenue to Stoke Wood for night parking.[196]

(opposite and following) 22. The centre of Exeter as it was before the war.

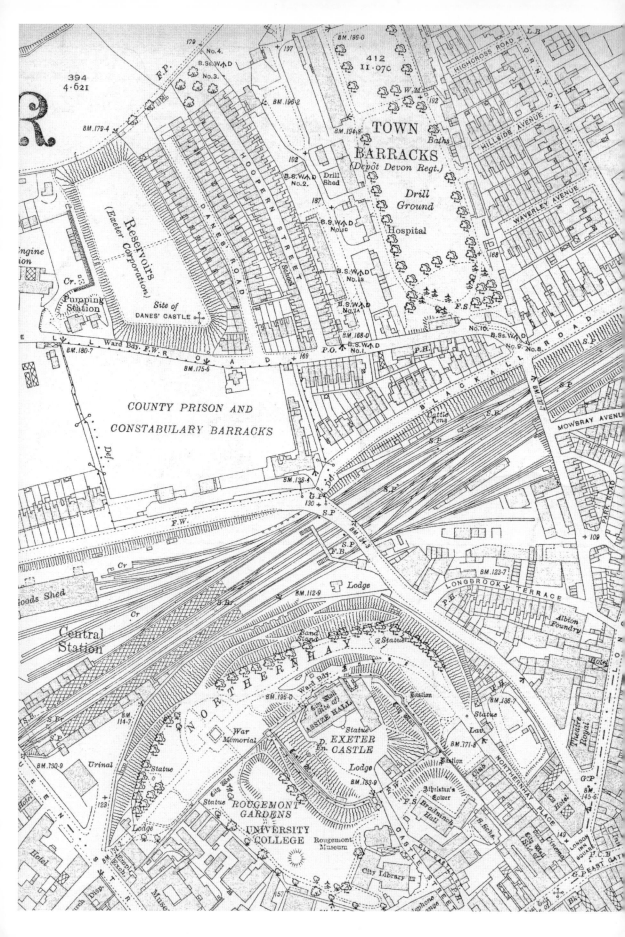

23. *Fire in the city.*

24. *Paris Street.*

25. Two firemen at work.

26. Tea for blitzed workers.

27. Food and drink being served following the blitz.

MAY

In the early hours of Monday, 4th of May, a devastating attack, remembered as the blitz, was made by the Luftwaffe. A few days afterwards the National Fire Service made a report:

The attack commenced at approximately 0136 hours and developed very rapidly, lasting until 0250 (1 hour and 14 minutes). The technique of the attack was, Incendiary Bombs followed by High Explosives, followed by further showers of Incendiary Bombs and High Explosives. It has been estimated by representatives from Princess Risborough, working in conjunction with the Air Ministry and the Local Police, that approximately 7,000 Incendiary Bombs and 150 High Explosives were dropped during this raid, and there is no doubt that the City centre was the objective. The nature of the property in the centre of the town with its many alleys and courts adjacent to the High Street, easily allowed the fires to get a hold and spread, not so much North and South of the main street, but to the East and West of it, making control very difficult, and further spreading almost impossible.

The fires were at times entirely across High Street, and in the case of Bedford Circus, it was never possible in the early stages to gain entrance to this Circus to attack the fires.

As a number of blocks of property were destroyed it is very difficult in this report to give authentic figures as to the

CITY OF EXETER

C. J. NEWMAN,
TOWN CLERK
AND
CLERK OF THE PEACE.

TELEPHONE NO. 4956
(3 LINES).

TOWN CLERK'S OFFICE,
EXETER.

May, 1942.

Dear Sir, or Madam,

It is with deep regret I have to inform you officially that

has been killed as the result of enemy action, and the City Council are arranging for burial at the Higher Cemetery, Pinhoe Road, Exeter, at   on

It will not be possible to arrange a Funeral Cortege from the City Mortuary, and I would, therefore, suggest that you and other relatives who are able to attend, should be at the Cemetery not later than   on

Yours faithfully,

Town Clerk.

28. The letter which was sent by the city regarding casualties in the bombing. Details were later filled in.

number of buildings and houses destroyed, although full details as far as it is possible to obtain I set out in Appendix 11, but as a brief summary I would suggest the following:

Destroyed by Fire and H.E.'s total 550
Damaged by Fire and H.E.'s total 620

During the raid a high wind appeared to spring up from South West, which considerable assisted the spreading of fires, although it can be safely stated that at 0640 hours the fires were under control.[197]

The King and Queen visited on May 8. An unexploded bomb was found on the train line before St David's Station shortly before they were due to arrive and dealt with. Elsewhere bombs were also found but these too were made safe. The royal couple toured the city and saw the great damage.

TC.CS.   29th June, 1942.

PRIVATE AND PERSONAL.

Dear Smith,

     Many thanks for your letter of the 27th instant and for the information you have kindly given me which I will of course pass to the Mayor in confidence. I am interested in what you say about Mr. Bennett as he gave me to understand that he had been a member of your staff.

     I am sorry to say that a large section of our High Street has completely disappeared, and except for a small portion, the old-world charm has disappeared for ever. Our total deaths for the three raids in April and May was 261, including missing, and I quite agree with you that the number of killed in all cases which I have heard seems surprisingly low having regard to the nature of the attack. I too wonder whether the same does not apply to our bombing of Germany.

     I am glad that you and your family are uninjured but it is bad enough to have your house damaged twice. I join you in wishing a speedy end to the whole horrible business.

     Heartily reciprocating your good wishes, and kindest regards,

               Yours sincerely,

Frederick Smith, Esq., B.A.,   Town Clerk.
The Council House,
COVENTRY.

29. *The letter sent by Exeter's town clerk to Coventry following the blitz.*

Among the places visited were the cathedral and the High Street. They were shown a piece of the bomb which hit the cathedral and the king was heard to say 'Send it for scrap'. The queen was said to have added 'that's right, let us send it back to the Germans'.[198]

The devastation created an extraordinary amount of paper work for the council staff and it took many years to complete. There were immediate letters such as those for compensation for goods; an Aylesbeare woman had left a child's panama hat to be cleaned at a firm in Paris Street and a navy blue pleated skirt at a Sidwell laundry while a student at St Luke's College wrote from his parent's home in Portsmouth of the loss of his clothes.[199] The Billeting Officer for Holsworthy also asked for verification that the homes of nine Exeter citizens, whom he had found accommodation

30. The Lower Market destroyed by bombing.

for as being homeless, were indeed destroyed by enemy action. Another man, from Minehead, enquired about the condition of a house in Leighton Terrace owned by his wife and added as a postscript 'I hope the old Guildhall still stands.'[200] The city itself was processing its own insurance claims. That for the City Library was eventually cleared for 33,157 lending library books destroyed as well as 62,300 titles in the reference library. Only 7,500 books had been evacuated. A compensation sum of £44,000 was agreed.[201]

On the 16th it was reported Bedford Circus was to be demolished 'to safeguard public safety and salvage'. However, four days later a letter was sent to the City Surveyor from Jacksons & Sons regarding 15a Bedford Circus. Their client had been advised it was not dangerous and did not understand why it was scheduled for demolition. They wrote 'Some reference seems to have been made to action by offices of HM Army but the city is not under Martial Law, and we shall be glad to have an explanation of the situation in the city.' Just before this it was pointed out to the town clerk that the Ministry of Works policy was that all historic and ornamental buildings should be preserved and it was presented with a list of damaged religious buildings including St Lawrence church.[202]

The tremendous number of meals was provided at Emergency Feeding Centres. At St Thomas Girls' School they provided 8,245 breakfasts, dinners,

31. Bedford Circus before the war.

teas and suppers from the 5th of May until the 12th. When charges began on the 8th the number of meals dropped from 1,338 on the 7th to only 578 the following day. Other centres included John Stocker Boys School which fed 980 in the same period, Exe Island School catered for 7,294, Holloway Street School 6,257, St James Girls' School 7,162, Bradley Rowe Girls' School 7,060, Heavitree School and Ladysmith School 9,126, Episcopal School 2,316, Whipton Junior School 4,060, Paul Street Central Kitchen 56,260 and Civic Hall British Restaurant 20,374. The Queen's Messenger Food Convoy provided 40,400 hot drinks, sandwiches, stews and soups.[203]

Finally, on the 26th members of the council stood in silent tribute to those who had died on the night of May 3–4.[204]

On the 5th of May the *Express & Echo* published a broadcast to the German people by Ernst Von Kugel, who claimed to be a pilot who had bombed Exeter.

'It was a night of horror for the people of Exeter. When I approached this town, the bright reflection of fires on the horizon guided me. Over the town itself I saw whole streets of houses on fire, flames bursting out of the windows and doors and devouring roofs. People were running everywhere, and firemen were frantically trying to deal with the fires. It was a fantastic, fascinating sight. No

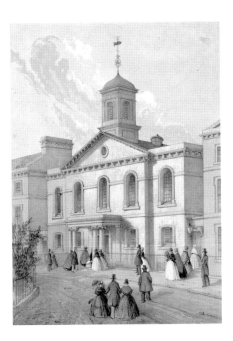

32. Bedford Chapel in about 1860.

one who saw it will forget the greatness of this disaster. While we circled the target of streets, my commander sighted a big stately house on the fringe of the sea of fire. At that he aimed – and hit it with a high-explosive bomb. The bomb burst and debris flew towards the sky, the force of the explosion rocking our plane. What destruction! We thought of the thousands of men, women and children, the victims of our deadly visit. But we thought, too, of our *Fuehrer*, and the word of command he gave: 'revenge!' With cool calculation we carried out our orders.'[205]

James Whiteside, the city's Information Officer, wrote an unusual account. He recorded that his brief was to keep the people of Exeter informed after heavy bombing. On the afternoon of May 3 he and his wife had gone to see bomb damage from the previous week and decided Exeter had finally had 'its turn'. In the evening he went to Culverland Road to see the last of the unexploded bombs:

An ugly thing – as big as a man. It had fallen in the side garden of a small house. The householder had an aviary and the bomb was buried in the ground within inches of a cage of Indian pheasants and other birds of bright plumage. The police had been feeding them with corn. Lucky birds, I thought. They did not like strangers, but seemed not to mind the bomb.

Unfortunately the worst was yet to come.

On that night I went to bed, tired and carefree. I heard no siren, but I dimly remember hearing the unmistakable urr-urr of a German aeroplane. I had heard the sound often enough before and I was not unduly worried by it.

I was really awakened by my son rushing into the bedroom shouting 'Incendiary Bomb!' I know that I dressed because I was in a dressed condition the next time I thought about it. I rushed outside and found incendiary bombs burning everywhere; my own I put out with sandbags (delivered free to every household by the local authority) and such others as I could see about me were in the street and in gardens and unlikely to cause much damage. My wife marshalled her mother (81) and three of our four children (13, 5, 4) into the hall of the house which had been strengthened as a refuge room (the courage of all of them was marvellous: I think that I was the only frightened member of the family). Our son (15) had disappeared: tin hat worn at an angle and stirrup pump trailing under one arm. (I learnt afterwards with pride that he had done some stout work: but this is my story, not his). By this time high explosive bombs were falling – and everything else too, as it seemed. I went out several times. People were scurrying about and I scurried about too, occasionally falling flat on our faces as planes dived low over us. Everyone seemed to be dealing adequately with his own incendiary bombs. Machine gunning was heard from time to time; but always the crash of explosives. I remember hearing one, two, three, four, five crumps with no explosions. Five in a row and pretty near and none of them exploded, I thought, and speedily forgot

about them. Ringing of fire engine bells; ambulance bells; shouting; bombs crashing; house shaking; glass breaking; machine gunning; havoc!

Quiteness! Again I went out. Fires some distance away but all seemed quiet near at hand. Then I saw that the house next door to mine was on fire. I do not know if I saw it or heard the crackling; but it was on fire. (My neighbour, unknown to me, had taken fright from the previous small air raids and had gone with his wife to sleep in the country)

Volunteers quickly gathered and in a few moments eleven stirrup pump parties were pumping water into the burning house. The flames grew in fury and, when the blessed 'All clear' sounded, the house was burning fiercely; flames caught by a strongish wind reaching out challengingly to my house only a few feet away. Volunteers were there in plenty, notably half a company of A.T.S. girls from a neighbouring hostel. (Taking these girls as a cross-section, I would assess the taste in pyjamas of our warrior girls at approximately six pink to four pale blue) And how these amateur fire-fighters and water carriers worked – but the battle was a losing one. It seemed that my house would surely take fire and I asked a few people to removed a few easy pieces of furniture from it. With gusto the girls swarmed into the place and, as it seemed, my house was stripped of every stick and stitch of furniture in a twinkling. Good work! (the rents in the wallpaper were not caused by attempts to removed that also, but by the Hercul-ean zeal of inexperienced furniture removers – a heavy wardrobe that took four men to take upstairs took a girl and a half to bring down, and in half the time) Fun! Of course it was! The girls loved it and I loved them for it. My wife and children were in a neighbour's house organising a running buffet. My furniture was piled up on the pavement and placed in nearby garages. And still the fire raged. And other fires roared. Fires all round us. And the sky overheard burned with a glow that could be seen for miles (in fact, over thirty miles).

The direction of the wind suddenly changed. I noticed it and many people to whom I have spoken since also noticed it. The wind changed and my home was no longer in danger. But the fire still raged and sweating blackened stirrup pump parties and water carriers were relieved by sometime furniture removers.

At length the flames subsided. The incendiary bombs had completed their dirty work. Dawn came and, with fewer helpers, my furniture was returned to the shelter of my roof – dumped. (as a matter of historical record, there was missing, presumably stolen, one torch, one toothbrush, and two rugs – also missing were all the buckets my wife had owned, but this loss can be understood.)

Rumour carriers were abroad: I heard that the cathedral had been destroyed; the Guildhall burnt out; High Street and Fore Street a mass of flames from one end to the other (Later in the day several people informed me that they had heard that I had been seriously injured and was in hospital).

Eureka! The scheme was beginning to work.

The point from which the Service was to operate was Hele's School. I cannot remember the devious route we followed to get there. Unexploded bombs and debris were everywhere. Shocks galore! But no foot-weary wandering by the homeless in search of rest. No panic. Not tears – yet. The city was excited and astir. We passed Culverland Road (either then or soon after) and I saw with regret that the house with the aviary that I had visited so long ago on the previous day had fallen with its neighbours: a direct hit from a high explosive bomb. The luck of the Indian pheasants had been short-lived.

And so to Hele's School with banner already flying – 'Information Centre' – in the bright morning sunshine. Some of the team had already assembled. One member informed me that since seven o'clock he had been giving impromptu announcements from a loud-speaker van in districts which had suffered no damage: warning people not to rush into the bombed areas and advising them to make ready to receive in their homes their friends who had been bombed out; telling the people that the fires had died down and that work of demolition and clearance and rescue was already in hand.

The paper scheme was taking practical shape.

One point in the scheme which we had thought a year ago to be rather elaborately far-sighted related to the production of 15,000 circulars of changed addresses and other items of information which we hoped to have printed for distribution on the first day of our operations. We had had the circular set up in type in skeleton form and the type left with a printer. We contemplated the possibility that this printer's works should be destroyed so we had a separate set of type set up and deposited it in the house of a member of the team who lived in a nearby village. We thought of the possibility that the circular would need to be printed out of Exeter. And it was so. The printing works where our type had been set up was demolished and all other printing works were out of action because of the cutting off of electricity. We speedily filled in such blanks in the skeleton circular as we could and our member rushed it off to Crediton – thence to Tiverton where he placed his order.

The Regional Information Officer, who attended at the Information Centre, informed me that he had arranged for six loud-speaker vans to be sent into Exeter in accordance with the scheme and we set about the preparation of a bulletin. We gathered such information as we could from the representatives of the many departments assembled at Hele's School and at 10.30 am, by which time the loudspeaker vans had arrived, our earliest 'official' messages were 'on the air'. The messages called attention to the existence and purpose of the Information Centre at Hele's School; the situation of the Emergency Feeding Centres and Food Office; traffic and post office arrangements. These announcements were made in every quarter of the city; they were rather scrappy, but more important than what they were was the fact of them. The people of Exeter were made to know that somebody was concerned to bring the news to them.

The scheme was working; but not without difficulty in running it. Decidedly more volunteers had been enrolled than were needed to conduct operations. The wisdom of this was seen during the morning. One 'key' man had been killed. Another came in pyjamas and

overcoat, ready to work but preferring not to do so: to his relief he was told that we could do without him – he was led gently by the hand to a spot a few yards away where he was given immediately some coupons wherewith to provide himself with some new clothes. Another had lost home and business; others, more elderly, were hardly fit physically or mentally for the strain that the work would put upon them. For most pressing business reasons, our typist was unable to come and the typewriting job fell to me. Several girls were roped in to do the job but al of them asserted that they would not type much. In each case the girl's estimate of her capacity erred on the side of over-praise.

At 2.30 pm a second and fuller bulletin was similarly broadcast; and at 7 pm a third and more full broadcast was made throughout the city. By 7 pm the 15,000 circulars had been delivered and were distributed in parcels to the many wardens' posts and by hand-to-hand from the loud-speaker vans – they were eagerly seized upon by the crowds. By any standard of criticism this circular was not a good one: but the fact of its issue in such short time was important. Three loud-speaker tours and a circular on the first day; the people were beginning to have confidence that efforts were being made to interpret to them what was being done. The scheme was working.

A word about the Information Centre at Hele's School – risen like a Phoenix from the ashes. Here were established representatives of 53 government, local authority and public utility departments: the idea being that every enquiry from the public would be dealt with under the one roof. This was truly 'Enquire within about Everything'. Thousands of people visited the Centre: thousands of enquiries were dealt with and thousands of pounds in immediate relief paid out by the Assistance Board, the Public Assistance Committee and the Mayor's Air Raid Relief Fund. Many volunteers offered their help and few were turned away. At the peak period no less than 510 people were fully employed in the Centre. A shuttle service of meals was instituted and everyone who worked in the place was fed in the place. There was no panic: no fuss: no officialdom: no delay: no scenes: no displays of bad temper. Queen's Messenger Food Convoy Vans were serving cups of tea and light meals in the adjacent Bury Meadow, and with the bright sunshine, the banners signifying the different departments (some of them operating form mobile vans in the grounds), the crowds, and the scurrying arm-banded messengers, a stranger would have been excused for thinking that he had encountered a gala occasion. The perfect running of the Centre cannot be over-praised. The co-ordinating officer was Mr Haley, the deputy city treasurer.

On the next day three more bulletins were issued – morning, afternoon and evening – and were broadcast in every part of the city from six loud-speaker vans. Again was the material for these bulletins collected from the representatives of the many departments at the Information Centre. The bulletins generally became more full and informative as I acquired a greater skill in preparing them and the announcers in uttering them – there is a technique in producing and announcing a bulletin by loud-speaker.

On this second day and thereafter about 200 copies of each bulletin were stencilled and circulated among Government and local government departments, public utility undertakings, police and wardens' services. In addition to the settled bulletins, further 'rush' announcements were made from time to time about matters of urgency not contained in the bulletins, or to allay particular rumours, or matter applicable only in certain districts. By this time our typist difficulty had been solved in a rather humorous way. I found two girls who had come into the Centre to look round but who were quite prepared to do a job. They were employed by the National War Savings Association (of the local Committee of which I was a member). They were expert typists and, *mirabile dictu* [wonderful to relate], were both expert in the use of the very complicated duplicating machines that had been delivered on that day. It appeared that their office had been bombed, but was in course of being removed to other premises and they had been given the day off while the removal was completed. The Emergency Information Officer set them to work with one hand and reached for his hat with the other. He went to see the Regional War Savings Organizer and by flattery, cajolery and scripture ('What are two among so many?') he secured them to him for the duration of the 'aftermath', subject to a day's notice to terminate the arrangement. The notice was not given and the girls did a grand job.

On this day I assembled all the skeleton placards which had been supplied to me by the Ministry of Information and which had been dispersed in five lots in different parts of the city. The poster 'For

Help and Information go to . . .' was overprinted 'Information Centre at Hele's School'; 'Boil your Water and Milk' was used, and additional posters about Rest Centres were produced. Bill-posters were found and 600 posters exhibited. No owners of poster sites have yet made any complaints or commenced any action for trespass . . .

Whiteside went on to write that on the second day a member of the National council for Social Services began work, from a converted horsebox, to support people on the eastern side of the city – there were no bridges across from Hele's School (now Exeter College) to High Street. After eleven days the centre closed.[206]

JUNE

The council was urgently trying to find accommodation for displaced traders. Recommended sites included Paul Street Car Park, Southernhay Greens, Trinity Green, Northernhay, Queen Street from the railway station to the clock tower, Belmont Pleasure Ground and the Bishop's Palace. There were also discussions within the council on the need to begin planning the rebuilding of central Exeter.[207] In the middle of the month the town clerk tried to obtain explosives in order to be more efficient in demolishing war-damaged buildings. Permission was refused.[208]

The City Surveyor reported allotments were damaged by air raids and arrangements were made to fill in bomb craters. Plaster from demolished houses was carted to Stoke Hill allotments.[209] It was reported Plymouth's Librarian had offered to return the books sent by Exeter when its own library was destroyed through bombing. The police reported their casualties in the blitz had been comparatively slight: two men hurt their spines, two others had slight injuries and one man had died. It also reported reinforcements had come from Devon, Plymouth and Somerset and they had been in the city for 15 days.[210] In the middle of the month the Buried Casualties Location Outfit searched premises at the top of Fore Street, South Street and Market Street and returned to the City Hospital where they used a special van with electrical equipment devised to find bodies.[211]

The council wrote to the King and Queen to thank them for their visit and to 'assure their majesties of the continued and unfailing loyalty of the citizens of Exeter'.[212] In June the town clerk expressed his gratitude for support: he wrote to the management and staff of Bobby's, Deller's Café, the Bude Restaurant, Imperial Hotel, Rougemont Hotel and the Great Western Hotel in appreciation of their 'splendid efforts' in providing emergency meals in the aftermath of the blitz.[213]

Insurance for the city's messenger boys was arranged: £250 would be paid as compensation in the event of loss of life or the loss of two limbs or two eyes, boys who suffered the loss of one limb or eye would be given £125 and any other permanent total disablement would merit a payment of £25 for up to ten years. The boys worked, generally on bicycles, five days a week from 9 am to 6 pm and on Saturdays from 9 until 1 pm.[214] Posters were distributed in the city with the titles 'If you are bombed out', 'This is a rest centre' and 'Fix thing up now'.[215]

JULY

The aftermath of the blitz overwhelmed local officials. For example, the Regional Salvage Officer approved the demolition of various properties including Swiss Cottage in Prince of Wales Road where the walls had to be removed to minimise the fire risk.[216] Also, the town clerk wrote to the managing director of the Rougemont Hotel that 'let us hope we shall never have to function again in such circumstances but if unhappily we do I am quite sure that the same willing cooperation will be manifest again'.[217] The city's librarian, Mr Tapley-Soper, tried to maintain petrol rationing so he could continue travelling from Topsham to work. He was told to find closer accommodation and the town clerk was not moved by his being over the age of retirement, disabled legs, having rheumatism in his hands and shoulders and unable, at nearly 17 stone, to take public transport.[218]

Further bombing was also a concern: a general circular and secret priority message was sent to all A.R.P. Controllers that there were three new types of German incendiary bombs.[219] Frictions were inevitably created by wartime restrictions. One example is a story told for several weeks in Exeter of an ambulance driver who was siphoning off petrol in order to give it to a young woman for her travels north to Mortehoe. The gossip began when another woman repeated it to her doctor.[220] More seriously, sweets began to be rationed.

AUGUST

At the beginning of the month the Inspector of Ancient Monuments wrote to the town clerk regarding the façade of the Commercial Union Offices at 238 High Street. He suggested it, along with its railings, should be saved given its historical importance. Although railings were needed for the war effort he wrote that the Chairman of the Appeal Tribunal had seen the

33. The Commercial Union Office on High Street can be seen on the left with the tower of St Stephen's church beyond it. The statue of King Alfred is just visible.

building and suggested he would give the matter a favourable consideration. The town clerk was against saving any part of the building and a few days later the Company wrote they only wanted the statue of King Alfred.[221]

There was a discussion at the Rotary Club on New Exeter. The President, Mr M. F. Mann, said if the council 'could retain an expert, a super architect, a man with a vision, to say what was wanted, that would be a first step.' Worries were expressed that vested interests would thwart development and there were comments the young men fighting the war should come home to decide on what the younger generation wanted. It was also discussed whether the High Street should be widened and that new buildings should be planned on the medieval character of the city. Finally, Bedford Circus was foreseen as the city's business centre.[222]

A report was completed on the amount of foodstuffs damaged by glass splinters and flying debris or destroyed in the bombings of April and May. An estimated 178,733 cans, packets or parcels of food were examined and seven tons were condemned.[223] Food was also on the mind of an employee of Barclay's Bank who wrote to the town clerk that he was not able to buy a cup of tea after 5.30 in the evening except at the British Restaurant at Exe Island or at the Rougemont Hotel. His hours at the bank were from 9 am until 5.30 to 6.00 pm whereupon he waited in the city until 8.30 when he was on duty fire-watching. He added it was not possible to find breakfast until after 9 am.[224] Other food news included the harvesting of the fifty acres of grain planted by the council.[225]

Several hundred men from the fire service paraded from Southernhay West through the High Street and back to their station at Howell Road.[226] In August the fire-watching scheme was extended to women aged between twenty and forty-five.[227] In a touch of irony, the new Control Centre of the A.R.P. moved from the city library to St Germans in Pennsylvania. The move had begun shortly after the blitz when much of the library was destroyed.[228] The Control Centre was inspected and it was concluded there was a general impression of untidiness: eighteen people slept there on an ordinary night (up to 30 during an Alert) and the single bathroom and lavatory for each sex was considered inadequate.[229]

This month at the Savoy Margaret Lockwood and James Mason appeared in *Alibi*, 'a sensation mystery thriller' set in 'gay Paris of 1937 with a background of sunny streets and glittering night clubs', while at the Odeon there was *Weekend in Havana* starring Alice Faye, Caesar Romero and Carmen Miranda. Meanwhile among the shows at the Theatre Royal were ballets presented by a company formed 'with the approval of the governments of the free peoples to keep alive the culture of the nations through the war'.[230]

Money was sent by neighbouring towns to help with the effects of bombings. The chairman of Crediton Urban Council gave a cheque for £485 to the mayor for the Air Raid Relief Fund. He said 'we have watched with great admiration the courage and bravery of your people of Exeter who, although losing all, have shown such a magnificent spirit to carry on'. The money was raised through house-to-house collections and several impromptu dances.[231]

The city's Postmaster informed staff they faced a threat from phosphorous and other new incendiary bombs which had a higher casualty rate than previous ones.[232] A report was made on Morrison table shelters in the middle of the month which noted the 'enemy's present policy of attacking the residential areas of medium and small-sized towns make imperative the immediate provision of all readily available forms of air raid shelters'. Exeter had at that time 9,469, an increase from May when there were only 5,918.[233]

SEPTEMBER

The destruction had caused a severe loss of retail buildings. For example,

Cadena Cafés Ltd was having difficulties with acquiring a lease on the City Hotel on Queen Street. The company, which owned Deller's Café, had expanded its smaller High Street café and was attempting to compensate for the loss of its main building but the American Red Cross was also vying for the City Hotel.[234]

Civil defence activities were varied. For example, Mrs Paddon, of Leighton Terrace, aged 64, finished her course in physical and recreational training for the A.R.P. This included Swedish Free Standing Exercises. Her instructors thought 'although blunt [she] will do well with any class as she makes so very plain what she it out for.'[235] There were concerns with security at the A.R.P. Control Centre: information regarding bombs, incidents and local alarms may have been given out to unauthorised persons either in person or over the telephone.[236]

OCTOBER

Battle of El Alamein and the Allied Offensive opened in Egypt. Freda Chappell of Ottery St Mary complained about the British Restaurant at 109 Fore Street. She claimed 'the potatoes served today were disgusting and looked fit for pigs only. They were partly mashed but consisted mostly of hard black pieces as large as a walnut. Eight of the eleven people sitting near us left every scrap, after the first mouthful. I understand it is now a punishable offence to waste, the person in charge of the cooking at this restaurant should get 12 months without delay, before ruining more good food. I did all the cooking for my own guest house for years, but I cannot think what they can do to make them look and taste as bad as these.'[237] An investigation followed on the quality of the food.

Accidents continued. One was reported by Mr C. A. Prophet of 8 Avondale Road: 'on Saturday night the 24th October, following an alert I was cycling along Magdalen Road on duty when I had the misfortune to collide with and knock down a Mrs Phyllis Brown. She was walking with a soldier companion in the road on the left hand side between Victoria Park Road and Marlborough Road towards the city, with their backs to traffic, whereas on the right hand side of the road there was a pavement. It was, or course, during blackout time. The lady has reported no personal injuries and at the time said she was all right, but she is now claiming for her coat which she says is absolutely ruined.'[238]

There were also further concerns of German bomb development. Four-pound anti-personnel bombs were being fitted with fuses which delayed detonation up to twenty minutes after impact. Exeter people were warned to wait at least 30 minutes before approaching any unexploded bombs.[239]

Rumours spread regarding scandalous comments allegedly made by the Fire Force Commander at a meeting in Exeter.[240]

NOVEMBER

The Allies made further gains in North Africa including Tobruk. In Exeter notes began circulating of remarks seen as inflammatory allegedly made at a firemen's meeting in October. A letter by the town clerk, marked 'Personal and Confidential' was sent to the regional office on the incident. It was of 'the greatest possible concern'. Nine points were reportedly made on the blitz: 1, the pipe line was all wrong – cause of fire in Exeter; 2, local knowledge no good or use; 3, local authorities can squeal; 4, as government paid they can dictate policy; 5, local authorities no voice or right; 6, forget about returning to local authority after war; 7, if Exeter do not want him, just too bad, Mr Morrison must find him a job; 8, police generally obstructive – would like to sack some of the tin pot chief constables. One at present giving lecture on blitz at which he was not present; 9, static water tanks outside councillors' houses. Over the course of the next few months it was suggested it was no longer possible for the fire official to work in Exeter.[241]

More complaints were made of the quality of food in local British Restaurants. One visitor from Paignton wrote that 'the place was dirty and the food compared with our English standard like one expects and gets in a slum eating house . . . for a shilling one received a portion of re-boiled and cold mash potatoes which were black, a very small portion of lukewarm mashed turnips, a piece of roast beef a quarter of the size of this paper and it was cold and tough and covered with gravy out of a cold jug standing on a wooden table. A small portion of completely indescribable fruit pudding completed this so-called meal. The only good thing I could see was the plates were clean'.[242]

The City War Emergency Committee gave £3 in compensation to H. E. Moore, a sixteen-year old A.R.P. messenger who lived in Oxford Road. The teenager's bicycle and Macintosh were stolen during the night of the blitz. He had left it in the care of a constable who watched another lad take it away.[243]

Requests were made to photograph the city's destruction. A corporal in the Royal Canadian Air Force was given permission on condition his photographs were not published, that they were not of buildings of military importance and that there was no detrimental effect on local security or to the war effort. Other requests were received from the rector of St James church, Whitton & Laing, Barclays Bank, Commercial Union and from the head of the School of Art.[244]

The city celebrated 'Civil Defence Day', a day of national remembrance and thanksgiving for the defeat of German air attacks from 1940 to 1941.[245] General public entertainment included a Boxing Tournament at Buller's Hall organised by the Exeter Amateur Boxing and Physical Training Club. B. Selby, 9 stone and 6 pounds, fought A. Wright, 12 stone and 10 pounds.[246] Miscellaneous occurrences included an increase of traffic in Goldsmith Street owing to a larger number of traders. The street was made one-way from the High Street to Paul Street.[247] Also, there was a change of use for the church of Allhallows-in-the-walls, which had been earmarked as an information centre. It was later used for making parachutes.[248]

December

After months of public discussion the council decided on the 15th to appoint a Standing Committee to begin planning the rebuilding of the centre.[249] One unexpected aspect of the war damage was an increase in vermin: the council had to renew the contract with a vermin destruction firm because mice had overrun a food store.[250]

Those who wanted to escape the war could see Vivian Leigh and Clark Gable in *Gone With the Wind*, Veronica Lake in *The Glass Key*, Milton Berle in *Whispering Ghosts* or Mickey Rooney in *A Yank at Eton*. 'Aladdin and His Lamp' opened on Boxing Day at the Theatre Royal. Among other attractions was the weekly dance at the Rougemont although one night the police stopped all those leaving in order to search their identity papers. It was a 'routine procedure'. Christmas food was difficult to buy: the market ran out of fish and shoppers were disappointed to discover the rumour of turkeys being available was false. There was even a queue for sprats. The mayor distributed dolls, books and animal toys to children whose homes had been bombed and gave them a celebration tea with food provided by well-wishers in Canada, the United States and South Africa.[251]

Five days after Christmas, on the 30th, there was a daylight raid by enemy bombers: at 10 am they 'caused certain amount of damage to dwelling houses and shop properties'. One rest centre was badly damaged and four others were opened for the public in different parts of the city. The roof spotter at the airport noted in his journal '10.05 – 10.35 three FW 190s firing machine guns, and shell bombs (6) also dropped – right on top of sirens. Buzzer pressed. One plane seen to fall in SW direction, one spitfire seen after reaching roof (fatal casualties in town)'.[252]

The number of deaths caused by the blitz in May was increased by one: a coroner's inquest in Lewisham ruled a local man, who had been visiting his sister in Exeter on the night of the blitz, died of injuries he had received that night.[253]

— 1943 —

JANUARY

The siege of Stalingrad was broken and the Russians began to move west. In Exeter the year was welcomed in with the comments 'Certain local happenings in the Old Year will live in the citizens' memory as long as memory lasts, and thereafter will have their place in history. Ravaged by the Nazis' methods of waging total war, the good old city raises her head more proudly than ever . . . and so we turn to 1943 hopefully and stout-heartedly, believing that at the very least it will being us a steadier stream of good news than have any of the war years that lie behind us.'[254]

The Home Guard's Exercise 'Gervaise' was held on the 3rd. It was to test the chain of command in a scenario in which serious casualties occurred to senior officers. The plans, marked Secret, envisioned large numbers of German parachutists, gliders and 'belly landing troops' having invaded Devon on the previous night and by 2 pm the following day there were reports of three columns at Okehampton Road, Old Okehampton Road and the road to Crediton. The Home Guard was in helmets and the 'Hun' in caps. The exercise concluded at 5 pm.[255]

Miscellaneous occurrences included efforts were being made to fix a defective water pipe at the Gras Lawn Allotments at the Princess Elizabeth Orthopaedic Hospital[256] and ten mobile canteens were operating in the city driven all, bar one, by women; the Women's Volunteer Service had two, the Salvation Army one and the Church Army seven.[257] There were continued claims for damage done to private homes by evacuee children: Mrs Burgoyne of 1 Cowick Road, for example, reported a mattress was ruined as well as six cups and saucers smashed.[258]

Radio continued to be important. In the middle of the month the town clerk announced on the Exeter Rediffusion Service 'In the future instead of an announcement you will hear in your rediffusion loudspeakers the actual sound of a siren giving you the 'alert' or the 'raiders passed' as the case may be'.[259] This month 'Home Flash', the radio programme for British Forces overseas, was hosted by Jan Stewer and came from Exeter.[260]

Included in the New Year's Honours list was Mr A. E. Rowsell, Exeter's Chief Constable, who was awarded an OBE.[261]

February

Fears of further bombings continued. On the 1st there were complaints of lights being seen in Topsham Barracks during blackout. Residents were alarmed.[262] A conference was held at Barton Hall where it was announced tip and run raids were expected to increase in coastal towns and villages.[263] There was a proposed increase in the provision of communal surface shelters. Some places set to have them were Victoria Road, Danes Road, James Street, Buddle Lane, Widgery Road and Shakespeare Road.[264] There were fourteen mobile canteens now in operation throughout the city.[265] At this time the Commanding Officer of the 36th Station Hospital of the U.S. Army wrote to the town clerk that he was maintaining 2 senior surgeons, 2 junior surgeons, 3 ambulances, 2 ¾ ton lorries, 20 nurses, 50 enlisted male medical attendants, 1 field kitchen, 1 field operating theatre, dressings and splints and 150 beds. The officer wrote that their services were available if needed.[266] Recent flooding at Heavitree Bridge and Sweetbrier Lane caused officials to remove the dam they had placed to create a reservoir of water for possible fire fighting.[267]

The council repaired homes damaged in April and May. One resident of Union Road expressed his thanks for making it possible for him to return home.[268] Efforts were also being made to help other places. For instance, the 'Help to London' Scheme brought in more donations from the South West Region than any other. Two three-ton lorry loads of more than 5,000 articles were sent: this comprised 268 articles of furniture, 385 of glass, 1,823 of china, 922 of kitchen utensils, 172 items of cutlery, 1,092 of linen, approximately 50 toys, 420 pictures and 50 miscellaneous items.[269]

March

On the 10th Noel Coward was taken ill with influenza and unable to appear in his play 'Present Laughter' at the Theatre Royal. Films on show included Vera Lynn at the Savoy in We'll Meet Again while at the Odeon there were Bob Hope, Bing Crosby and Dorothy Lamour in The Road to Morocco.[270]

There was an attempt to assess how many of the 250 daily dinners served at the British Restaurant in the Civic Hall up to the blitz had been to local people. A reply was made that originally the Civic Hall had opened as the

Evacuee Centre but had later changed its name to the British Restaurant. At first only some twenty per cent of the meals were for local people but once advertised this had climbed to some 75 per cent of the customers.[271]

Miscellaneous events included an accident on Ladysmith Road where an International Van knocked over Mrs Mary Ward, a pedestrian,[272] and residents of Bennett's Square in Whipton petitioned for two static water tanks.[273]

April

There were continuing concerns over future bombings. A petition was handed to the council by inhabitants of the Port View Estate in Heavitree regarding the overnight parking of omnibuses on Barrack Road. It was felt they were 'a good target for enemy aircraft'. The council reduced the number of vehicles and placed the others throughout the city.[274] Meanwhile, residents who lived near Polsloe Bridge complained the Air Raid Warning was not loud enough.[275]

The Red Cross wrote to the town clerk asking for help in publicizing the plight of 150,000 British, Dominion and Indian soldiers, sailors and airmen, merchant seamen and civilian internees on the continent.[276] Moves began to be made to provide facilities for British men and women in the armed services similar to those the Americans had in Exeter. The issue rumbled on through the autumn and was not settled until the end of the year.[277]

Vehicles used by the Emergency Services included, for the motor cycle messenger service, one Sunbeam, one Velocette and two Royal Enfields. There were also six first aid party cars; these comprised two Standards, a Humber 27, a Daimler, an Austin and a Hillman. Finally, there were problems with drivers who were using civil defence vehicles in obtaining petrol.[278]

May

Nationally, part-time work for all women aged between 18 and 45 became compulsory and the Allies won Tunisia. In Exeter a report was made of all shelters which showed a total of 147 communal shelters for 8,092 people, 9,104 Morrison shelters for 22,810, 11 two tier shelters for 55, 1,290 Anderson shelters for 7,740, 1,160 refuge rooms for 5,220 and public shelters for 5,308. Altogether they could accommodate 49,225 people.[279] On the 21st a fatal accident occurred at the Barley Mount static water supply tank. For many months there were concerns children were covering the netting with rubbish and causing damage. On that afternoon, at 4.30, David Terence Hoer, not yet five years old, was allowed out of his house to play and two hours later his mother found him drowned in the tank.[280] Six months before there was a campaign to stop the 'scandalous' damage being done to tanks. New regulations allowed fines up to £100 and 3 months' imprisonment but this did not save the child's life.[281]

There were three events in May. First, the Home Guard held a public parade to mark their third anniversary. The mayor said 'it was a day we shall all remember when this tragic war is only an unpleasant memory'. In a letter later sent to the men Lieut. Col. J. W. Western quoted Churchill's remarks regarding Dunkirk: 'we shall not flag or fail, we shall go on to the end'. He concluded 'Let the inspiration given us on Sunday last therefore urge us to carry on with cheerfulness and determination until the enemy has been completely smashed'.[282] Secondly, on the 25th the city celebrated the 'Wings for Victory' week with a parade.[283] Finally, there was a campaign against venereal disease: a film entitled 'subject for discussion' was shown at the Odeon and the Savoy over 6 days.[284]

Miscellaneous occurrences included a wireless being installed in the British Restaurant on Exe Island. They were popular because of their good value.[285]

JUNE

It was reported the Wings for Victory Week exceeded its target of raising £750,000; at least £885,708 was given. The common refrain was 'we must not let our airmen down'.[286] General Lindsay, the Deputy Regional Commissioner of the A.R.P., met training officers at Exeter and told them he 'hoped that when Armistice Day arrives it will still be our first place to help whatever government is in power to bring about and hammer out some sort of water-tight peace, and that satisfactory peace terms will be arranged so that we can look forward to enjoying the next 25 years instead of living in a fool's paradise as we had during the last'. Afterwards he introduced an American soldier who gave a lecture on the organisation of the American forces.[287]

In Exeter 16,644 new ration books were issued but 2,546 had still to be collected. An article was printed in the *Express & Echo* with the headline 'Are women as good as men – divided opinion'. One politician proposed council policy should be women were hired on a temporary basis only but Mr E. Pedlar objected. He argued women were as good in their jobs as men and they should not be denied permanent appointments because they were women.[288] On the 10th an Armstrong Siddeley, which operated

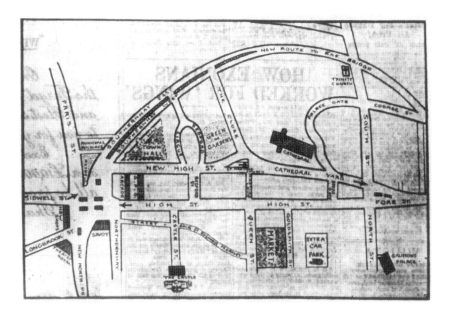

34. A sketch drawn by 'a citizen' of a plan for rebuilding the city, 5 June 1943.

as a first aid car, collided with a lamp standard at the junction of Hamlin Lane and Pinhoe Road. There were questions over liability.[289]

JULY

The Allies invaded Sicily. In Exeter miscellaneous events included the Chief Constable was asked to send a constable to the Stoke Hill Allotments on a Sunday afternoon to stop thefts, the civil defence services were told they needed instruction in the danger of anti-personnel mines[290] and William Charles Back of 46 Radford Road pleaded not guilty to a charge of deserting his fire-watching post on June 25 at the Higher Market. He argued he had attended from 10 to 12 pm but found his bedding had not been washed in over a year, was constantly in use and was infested with bugs. He returned home after making appropriate complaints.[291]

There was also concern over damage to graves in St Thomas caused by German bombing. Over the next few weeks a crater was filled in. Agreement was reached on housing 47 A.T.S. girls at St David's Institute Rest Centre. In the midst of the war effort, the town clerk demanded one worker pay for a personal phone call made in June, which lasted 16 minutes, at the A.R.P. Control Centre.[292]

Just over a year after Exeter's blitz there was an exhibition at the museum entitled 'On the Target' organised by the Ministry of Information. It featured photographs of bombings of Germany and enemy-occupied countries. The *Express & Echo* commented the 'evidence of destruction' was awful but thought there were two messages: one was of the valour of the Allied aircrews and the second was that it gave hope the destruction would save millions of lives. Bob Hope made a surprise visit to the city and signed autographs. The Wild West featured at the Theatre Royal with 'Ride em cowboy!'; it featured Pat O'Brien, the screen and radio star. There was also a public meeting on the Communist Party Congress.[293]

AUGUST

Sicily was won for the Allies and the bombing of the Italian mainland was continued. In Exeter a course of lectures on gas attacks was given to the Control Centre staff[294] and two boys broke open a public lavatory door at Topsham and stole two shillings and eight pence. When they were apprehended one was heard to say 'Us be caught'. Also in August a 17-year-old boy was bound over for stealing and given an ultimatum by a judge: find work or face imprisonment. He was told 'You are work-shy, and in these days there is no room for people who will not work. We are not going to stand any more of this nonsense'.

The government had a campaign to try to stop unnecessary travelling for summer holidays. In Exeter 'Holidays at Home' attempted to make up for children not being able to go away. Among the events was a fancy dress competition in Northernhay. James Cagney was in *Yankee Doodle Dandy* at the Savoy and the Flutterbyes appeared at night in Northernhay Garden.[295]

SEPTEMBER

The Allies invaded Italy. In Exeter the number of civil defence personnel stood at 1,266 general wardens, excluding fire-wardens, of whom 958 were men and 308 were women, and 74 shelter wardens, of whom 49 were men and 25 were women. There were 248 men in the Rescue services, 102 in Decontamination, and 91 messengers. The only women were in Report and Control which had 32 along with 9 men. In September the fire-watching scheme was extended to men aged between sixteen and sixty-three.[296]

An official complaint was made to Bobby's Restaurant after a customer was refused a roast beef dinner. He was told the management's policy restricted particular meals to long-standing customers. The man had been a customer for only six to seven months.[297]

There was a request to camouflage the cattle market, which was then being occupied by the U.S. Army. The market had been treated before but the colouring had worn away.[298] Bombing was still a concern.

October

A report was given to the council at the beginning of the month on plans to billet American troops in Exeter. The city agreed to provide two areas, near St James Park and near the County Ground, for 500 troops. The military was to see to its own beds and bedding. Also, other American servicemen would have non-compulsory billeting where there was already a male in residence and for lodging only. Finally, no 'coloured' troops were to be billeted.[299]

Moves towards rebuilding continued. The Replanning Committee reported they had chosen Thomas Sharp as consultant. He accepted the position and it was reported he would begin work immediately.[300] There was friction over the saving of old buildings. The Ministry of Works proposed that part of St George's wall, revealed by the bombing, should be saved because it was Saxon. It would cost an estimated £75. The town clerk was not in favour.[301]

A list was made of the motor vehicles to be used by the emergency services. Among them was one Arrol Astor, two Sunbeams, eight Austins, one Wolseley, two Daimlers and two Thornycrofts used as ambulances. A student of the University College wanted to contribute to the war effort and offered her services as a volunteer telephonist for the control centre but the town clerk turned down her application.[302]

November

Exeter's Clerk wrote he was against saving the Saxon fabric of St George's church because it would hinder his reconstruction plans and be a 'gross waste of public money'.[303] The issue of historic buildings continued with a letter from the Inspector of Ancient Monuments about Bedford Chapel, the early nineteenth-century building built near Bedford Circus by public subscription in 1832. He wrote:

. . . I discussed that burnt-out building with the Bishop of Exeter, he was, as I understood it, clearly in favour of retaining the remains, with a view to eventual rebuilding and reuse for ecclesiastical purposes. That may or may not be his present view, but without discussing the matter further with the ecclesiastical authorities, we hardly feel justified in removing the entry out of hand from our list of Historic Buildings.'

The Inspector stressed the importance of ancient buildings:

'A few remarks on the general matter of historic buildings in the devastated areas may here be pertinent. As you yourself have agreed, Exeter owes not a little of its renown and prosperity to its antiquity. This is reflected in many of its buildings. It does not seem right to us that any of them should be removed without due consideration, however badly it has been damaged by enemy action, if historic features remain. In such matters there are bound to be questions of degree. Bampfylde House was demolished by agreement between all concerned. Other buildings or walls have been left standing by the City Engineer in full collaboration with us, and we, as labour conditions permit, are gradually working on them with the consent of the owners and the money of the War Damage Commission, to arrest their deterioration until a final decision on their future can be taken. I, for one, freely admit that it may not be possible to retain them all during replanning, but you will, I hope, agree that in such a city as Exeter historical considerations should be given due weight with other considerations before the final verdict is pronounced. We do endeavour to be practical men as well as enthusiasts, and experiences of other devastated cities does not suggest that the conflicts of opinion will be many.

With all this in view, may I ask for your assistance in one matter? I understand that American soldiers are removing debris from the devastated areas for hardcore. There is a real danger that they may, inadvertently or otherwise, damage or even remove parts of some of the ruined Historic Buildings, such as the wall of St George's Church, which looks unimpressive, but is the oldest masonry above ground in Exeter, the Old Black Lion (South Street) and others. If you can contrive to guide them away from such a course of action, we shall be most grateful. We shall naturally do our best, by notices, etc., to the same end.'[304]

Developments in civil defence included local government officials digesting a secret report sent from Westminster regarding a recent London bombing raid: the police were criticised for not dealing with traffic and it was suggested other parts of the country needed to learn lessons from policemen who were too keen to help victims instead of carrying out their duties. At ten a.m. on the first Monday in November, and each month following, public warning sirens were tested for their mechanical efficiency. First the 'raiders passed' sound called, then the 'alert' and then finally the 'raiders passed' call. There was a demonstration of fire-fighting appliances and equipment at Dane's Castle.[305]

The town clerk wrote to the Misses Holmes at 24 Belgrave Road and informed them 'I am writing to you with reference to the serious position you are in respect of the above property. A careful inspection has been made and it is found that the house is in a very dangerous condition and liable to collapse at any moment'.[306]

Near the end of the month, on the 25th, some 2,000 American troops, clad in khaki, celebrated Thanksgiving in the cathedral.[307]

December

The city's clerk continued his dispute with the government's Inspector of Ancient Monuments. They were, he wrote, entirely in agreement regarding the importance of old buildings and that other officials were looking after the issue of the removal of debris but the main point of his letter was one of extraordinary deception:

The real difficulty of course is the definition of 'historic buildings' and it is for this reason that I mentioned the Bedford Church as it is quite news to me that this Church was ever regarded as an historic building. The fact that the Bishop may wish to retain the remains for use in future rebuilding is, of course, quite another matter that deserves every sympathy but I am quite at a loss to understand why this should justify it being designated by your Department as an historic building when, so far as I am aware, it has no claim whatever to be so regarded.

If other similar buildings are to be treated in the same way without any real justification, then I can only repeat there is bound to be controversy and a reaction of local public opinion which may result in the destruction of some things which certainly ought to be preserved in the interests of the City and of the Nation.

You also mention the wall of St George's Church and as you are probably aware, my Committee have expressed very strong views against the proposal to spend public money on the preservation of the wall which would seriously restrict the proper replanning of this devastated area.[308]

It is extraordinary the town clerk professed not to know that there had recently been a campaign by the Society for the Protection of Ancient Buildings which saved Bedford Chapel from demolition. In the 1930s they won their case and imagined they had secured the future of the building. Mr Newman had been in post as town clerk since 1929.

The Allied Services Club was to close at the Civic Hall and reopen at the Royal Albert Memorial Museum in rooms recently vacated by a government department. The club had on the ground floor two large rooms, a kitchen, store and office and on the first floor a large room for cards, a second room for billiards and a third for other games.[309] There was also continuing discussion on how to integrate U.S. surgical teams with the region's hospitals during emergencies. Each team had one surgeon, 1 assistant surgeon, 1 anaesthetist, two nurses and 8 medical orderlies.[310] A new Group of the Housewives Service began. In total there were 2,466 local women and there was a celebration to mark the new members with a training play and a 'novel item' which was 'the appearance of an old lady from the country who, in dialect, described in humorous vein how the Housewives Service was run in her village'. In spite of the bad weather and an outbreak of influenza there was an audience of 130 people. In December there was also a fatal accident: a bus hit a five-year-old boy while crossing a street. A shelter had obscured the driver's view. A member of the W.V.S. brought 'a very badly crippled girl' to Gloucester where she was given a test as a telephone operator but it was reported she was too infirm and they returned to Exeter.[311]

— 1944 —

JANUARY

This year's Theatre Royal pantomime was 'Cinderella'. Various seasonal entertainments were on offer including one organised by a section of the Housewives Service. They held a social and entertainment featuring an opera burlesque, monologues and songs by Jan Stewer. Another group had a party for members' children, each of whom was given a bag of sweets (provided by the American Red Cross) and the 'outstanding feature' were tinned peaches given by an American who was billeted with the Head Housewife. Agreement was reached amongst volunteers at the Allied Services Club Canteen: the Co-operative Group were on duty Monday nights from 6.30 to 10 pm, the Rotary Ladies on Tuesday nights, the Soropo-mists on Wednesday and the W.V.S. for the remaining evenings. There was general discussion whether women should be allowed free access to the Club and it was decided they could be allowed in the canteen and in the games rooms except for the Reading Room which was exclusively for men.[312]

Discussions continued into the case of a woman from 20 St John's Road. She was accused of being derelict in her first aid duties. For nearly a year local officials had tried to force her to work but she claimed she needed to look after her husband and daughter. Her workmates at the first aid post were not supportive; they claimed she and her daughter 'are able to attend dances and go to parties up until the early hours of the morning'. Moreover, the excuse she gave to an official was she had 'reached a certain stage in life'. She unsuccessfully suggested her work at the canteen at the American Red Cross at Mardon Hall took precedent. One official wrote of her, and her daughter, 'I am convinced they are slackers'.[313] Among other things, the facility at Mardon Hall for recuperating American servicemen was known for the used contraceptive devices which littered the adjacent grounds in the mornings.

Official papers show strict regulations were posted for breakfast at the Control Centre at St Germans House in the Messenger Room: at 7.40 am there was to be a preliminary warning bell, at 8 am porridge was to be served followed five minutes later by a second course. No breakfasts were allowed to be placed aside to be kept warm.[314]

February

The Civil Defence Regional Headquarters informed the town clerk, in a letter marked 'most secret', that 'military preparations and operations in this country may invite attacks from the enemy on an intensive scale, particularly in certain coastal towns and special targets'. It was proposed that some rescue services would be withdrawn, leaving Exeter with 13 parties and 159 men. It was also suggested that U.S. troops could take on any tasks which could not be undertaken by their British counterparts. The 102 Cavalry was based at Hele's School.[315]

This month discussions were held regarding what arrangements could be made for permanent allotments once the war ended[316] and the council began planning the building of some 2,000 homes and discussed plans for another 2,500 to 3,000 more.[317]

The work of the W.V.S. included serving at the British Restaurant, the canteen at the Royal Observer Corps and the Allied Services Club. One member helped the Jewish Refugee Association trace any children billeted locally with a view to arranging their religious instruction was not neglected. A small posy of flowers, in the colours of Poland, was sent on the birth of a Polish Flight Sergeant's baby girl. The Service also accepted a gift of 400 doughnuts from the American Red Cross (which had arrived too late for a football match) and these were distributed to local schools. The Housewives Service was also involved in doughnuts: it was asked to serve light refreshments to American troops at the 'Doughnut Dugout'.[318]

Public entertainment included Bette Davis in *Now Voyager* at the Savoy, Ginger Rogers in *Bachelor Mother* at the Odeon and Barbara Stanwyck in *Flesh & Fantasy*. At the Civic Hall a 'super non-stop' dance featured The Cherokees' Dance Band with a slow fox trot competition.

The Bishop made public comments that the country faced a new threat: after being threatened with invasion he felt that lust was now the new enemy.[319] He may have been referring to the licentious behaviour of some Exeter women with American soldiers. Residents have remembered local girls being brought by American servicemen into Northernhay at night for 'courting' or the popularity of the shrubbery around Mardon Hall also used by the Americans. Some months before a speaker in Exeter at the Church of England's Moral Welfare Council had commented that during wartime morals were an early casualty and pointed to evidence suggesting there were 'widespread loose morals'.[320]

MARCH

There was a complaint that Alerts were not announced at public entertainment events: a mother wrote to the town clerk that her daughter had attended a dance at the Civic Hall but was unaware of an Alert. When a public Alert had sounded in the streets the A.R.P. had suggested cinema managers place a message on the screen that 'The public sirens have just sounded the 'Alert' but this does not necessarily mean that a raid will take place. The performance will be continued but those who wish to leave should do so now and may take refuge in one of the public shelters nearby, the audience is, however, recommended to remain where they are'.[321]

This month the town clerk wrote to his Hastings counterpart regarding the aftermath of Exeter's blitz. He recounted some 5,000 'trekkers' had left each evening, slept in fields and then returned in the morning. He thought numbers increased because of fine weather and wondered whether a sudden change of weather was responsible for a drop in evacuees. He also noted that after the April raids the local bus company had run extra buses to meet demand but the police had stopped it and threatened drivers of private cars with prosecution for misuse of petrol. He stressed the authorities gave no assistance to those who fled.[322]

Compensation claims for war damages continued to be received, filled in and sent to insurers. The city claimed £500 for ten large oil paintings which were in the ballroom at the City Hospital. The pictures were portraits of George I, Sir Edward Seward (by William Gandy), an unknown architect, the second governor of the guardians and six members of the Bury family. Each painting was said to have been 250 years old.[323]

Among miscellaneous occurrences was that the W.V.S. provided a guide for three Canadian Air Force Officers who wanted to see the cathedral and guildhall. It was also reported in the *Express & Echo* that a 24-year-old soldier had written home with his opinion he hoped the future Exeter would be 'more modernly designed than the pre-blitz city he remembers'.[324]

APRIL

From the first of the month the city was in a Military Protected Area which extended from the Wash to Land's End and was some ten miles deep from the coast. Travel was prohibited to non-residents with few exceptions.[325] This was in response to the imminent invasion of France by the Allies.

Miss Ethel Lega-Weekes, the formidable local historian, rallied support to keep the Saxon fragment of St George's church. She wrote a wreath had been left on the wall by a well-wisher and referred to a recent letter in the *Express & Echo* from an American officer who had hinted there might be American funds to re-erect South Gate. She questioned whether there might just as well be support to preserve the church wall.[326]

The Social Welfare Committee collected 197 clothing coupons from its 46 staff. Nearly all were unmarried women.[327] The Chief Constable spoke to a meeting of the Housewives Service on the topic of 'Security'. He stressed the importance of not giving scraps of conversation to the enemy which might prove valuable. There was also a lecture on 'Women of Russia'.[328] Among the work of the W.V.S. was cooking at 3 Home Guard Exercises which involved open fires, attending a reception for members of the Canadian and American forces and knitting garments which were sent to the Merchant Navy, the Devons, Indian prisoners and the A.T.S.[329]

MAY

Digging for Victory was widespread although the Salter's Road Allotments suffered thefts. The War Departmental Land Agent wrote land was needed at the abattoir site for vital purposes with the war. It was noted with regret that the allotments there were then in full cultivation. The Stoke Hill Allotments were also under threat: it was announced the land was needed for housing.[330]

There was concern that frost could damage public air raid sirens,[331] a two-hour phosphorous bomb exercise was held in the city,[332] and the Ministry of Information sent supplies of 'You Have A House' and 'Ask A Policeman', posters which were to be used after a severe raid.[333] The W.V.S. reported their 'outstanding event' was the first day of the clothing exchange on the 23rd: it was open every Tuesday afternoon and was instantly popular. The Housewives Service held a firebombing exercise and it was said two members 'took the parts of hysterical women very realistically'. The group knitted a considerable number of garments including 34 white vests, 7 anklets and 11 scarves.[334]

The Home Guard celebrated their fourth year with a ceremony at the cathedral: the men marched from Exeter School. The occasion caused a sharp exchange of words between the chief constable and town clerk. The two men disagreed over whether the mayor should have an honorary police escort. A week after the event the chief constable wrote to say arrangements had changed after 25 years in which the mayor had always had a police escort. The town clerk responded 'I think it would avoid misunderstanding and waste of time if you would refrain from expressing views on a matter which is not in your province and which obviously you do not understand.' He stressed the occasion was only 'semi-state' and not requiring a large police presence. The chief constable had the final word: he asserted any police escort lay within his jurisdiction and added 'I have no desire to waste time and as your letter is discourteous any further communication I may wish to make I shall address elsewhere.'[335]

JUNE

On the 6th the Allies invaded France at Normandy. One resident of Exeter remembered the American servicemen in Exeter. Christine Caldwell was one of the students of the Central School of Speech and Drama which was evacuated to the city in September 1939. She later recalled 'there was a great build-up of American troops in the city and they were billeted in buildings throughout Exeter. One group of American sergeants lived in a house in Blackall Road and they played softball in the traffic-free street. One night my husband and I entertained these Americans but we had little to give them for supper except vegetables and some cheese so we gave them a great salad and I overheard one of the boys say under his breath 'What does she think we are? Rabbits?' Residents of Exeter had grown accustomed to hearing the Dakotas each night circling the city at the same time but when that suddenly ceased there was speculation that the long-anticipated invasion of France was about to begin. The Americans suddenly disappeared and the following morning we found belongings that they couldn't take with them, such as towels and packets of Jello, left for us on the garden wall of our house. Just before then one of the Sergeants from the Bronx had asked me if I had an atlas because he said he had often wondered where Cherbourg was. We found out later that was where he had landed.'

This month the Allies also entered Rome and the first V1 bomb fell in Britain. A note marked 'Strictly confidential' informed A.R.P. staff that code words were changed for messages sent to Bristol to inform the Regional Headquarters of enemy flights over Exeter: Bigben was to be used for rocket bombs and 'Diver' for pilotless aircraft.[336]

This month permission was granted to John Broom of 11 North Street to make paintings and sketches of ruined buildings in the city.[337] On the 15th at 1.30 in the morning there was an accident at Buddle Lane. Jimmy MacNamara, of the US Naval Air Force at Dunkeswell, was sheltering in a house during an air raid and had just parked his navy truck on the side of the road when Ronald Albert Orchard left his First Aid Post and collided with it while on his bicycle. Orchard suffered multiple cuts to his forehead and eyelid, broke his spectacles and damaged his bicycle. His compensation claim for just over £8 was paid a few months later.[338]

JULY

Exeter celebrated 'Salute the Soldier' Week from the 8th to the 15th with a parade.[339] The city was still off limits to visitors, except for a few exceptions, because it was in the Coastal Ban. The town clerk received letters from people attempting to avoid the restrictions including one Miss Richardson of Surrey who wanted digs in Exeter because 'flying planes are overhead of the house night and day and we get very little rest and the strain is getting me down'. She was refused permission to visit as were many others including an official from Lloyd's Bank in Worcester who appeared to be an old golfing friend of the town clerk's. He was informed he, and his son, would be turned away at St David's Station and was told the police had already done the same to hundreds, if not thousands, of others.[340]

Fifty-nine residents of the area around Bartholomew Street petitioned for the catacombs to be used as a shelter. A meeting was arranged and one resident apologised for wearing his 'working clothes' in front of the City War Emergency Committee; he had come straight from work. The committee voted against the proposal on the grounds a heavy high incendiary bomb near the entrance would bring down the roof. Some nearby houses had Morrison shelters, such as 18 The Mint which had seven residents, but locals felt safer in the catacombs. The issue had been discussed in 1942 and 1943. In July 1942 it was used by as many as fifty people but the surveyor's department wrote that 'during alerts [they] are now abusing this privilege'. It was suggested either a lavatory was installed or the gates could be locked to prevent public access.[341] Morrison shelters received a favourable report sometime after they had been in place in the city; one writer noted five very successful incidents in which they saved local lives. In an incident at Monks Road a high incendiary bomb created a crater of some 34 feet in diameter and 12 feet deep and the shelter was blown across the street over a communal brick shelter onto the house opposite. A woman and her two children were protected although unfortunately the child was hospitalised and later died from injuries received.[342]

AUGUST

Paris was liberated. In Exeter a dispute continued regarding payment for a coffin used to bury a local woman. She had died in Holloway Street during the blitz and her body, which was described as being 'in a very bad state', was placed in a coffin at the mortuary and not removed from it when collected for burial outside the city. The firm which transported the body would not pay the bill of £3 5s because it argued that it had not ordered that particular coffin.[343]

SEPTEMBER

Brussels and Antwerp were liberated and the first V2 bombs fell in Britain. In Exeter the total number of boys employed as unpaid messengers in the city's civil defence stood at 85. In general there was a relaxation by the government of civil defence duties. In Exeter the sleeping-in arrangements were discontinued for all but the permanent staff of the Control Centre.[344] There was also fewer restrictions on war reporting: the Chief Press Censor wrote, in a letter marked private and confidential, that more information could be given on air raids before 29th of February if it did not endanger security. The city celebrated 'Battle of Britain' Sunday on the 17th with a service at the cathedral and a parade of the armed forces and civil defence services.[345] Civil defence staff presented gifts to the town clerk and city treasurer. The latter thanked them: 'I shall never forget the courage and devotion to duty you all displayed, and, without which I should not have been able to go my own little part'. The number of evacuees dropped from 4,005 on the 2nd to 3,567 two weeks later.[346]

October

British troops landed in Greece and Athens was taken. In Exeter the war effort continued to be wound down. The number of Rest Centres was reduced by two thirds: Emmanuel Hall accommodated 250 people, the museum 500, Lopes Hall 120, Whipton Huts 85, St Lawrence Home 160, City Mission 200 and Reed Hall 300. Altogether these seven Rest Centres seated 1,615 people. There was also a reduction in first aid provision: at the end of the month two fixed first aid posts were closed as well as one more a fortnight later along with a heavy mobile unit.[347]

A report was made into the collection of indoor Morrison shelters. The public had made 5,147 offers to surrender them including by 168 persons who needed assistance to dismantle, 432 shelters had been collected and the remaining 821 were being collected as and when transport was made available. 1,282 shelters were dispatched to other local authorities, 4,041 shelters were stored at the Highway Depot and 842 returned incomplete of which 476 owners had given satisfactory explanations or returned missing parts.[348] Collection went on for months and comments were continually made such as that the Morrison shelter at 73 Oxford Road had its mesh panels removed for use as a garden fence.[349] Trivial paperwork continued to be filled in. This month the town clerk disputed with the Regional Office of the A.R.P. his payment claim for a driver.[350]

Plans were made for local women to be included in a public event for female members of the civil defence and kindred services in London. Miss Betty Francis Caddy, 26, was suggested because of her outstanding duty in organising the mortuary service during the blitz. The Queen presided and said 'I believe strongly that, when future generations look back on this most terrible war, they will recognise as one of its chief features the degree to which women were actively concerned in it. I do not think it is any exaggeration to say that, in this country at any rate, the war could not have been won without their help.'[351]

November

On the 14th the government announced the Home Guard would stand down.[352] General George Lindsay, at A.R.P. Regional Headquarters in Bristol, thanked the town clerk for recent hospitality. Lindsay reflected 'Another outstanding impression has been the fundamental unity of the British people in war and the way in which people of all classes, creeds and religious persuasions worked together as a team in face of enemy action . . . It is your duty to ensure that we retain that 'United Front' in the post war era for, believe me, we shall lose the peace if we do not'.[353]

A report was made by Kay Goddard of the Exeter W.V.S. which provides a fair idea of the war effort being made by women:

1. Ministry of Health nightdresses have been made, also 12 frocks from American Red Cross material.

2a. Evacuated school children are still being clothed under the L.C.C. scheme.

2b. Thirteen cases were dealt with during the month, and 297 coupons taken. The clothing department has been very busy checking up and sorting the different varieties of clothing in the depot.

3a. Meetings have been held in all Housewives Groups to explain the situation and position of the service in Exeter, and to inform all members that they should not disband. Everyone was most keen and ready to help in any way possible. Knitting afternoons have been held, and well attended, 76 garments being knitted and two nightdresses made up. The Allied Services Club Canteen team is still operating at full strength, also the Saturday night Information Bureau Team. Housewives have been asked to help at the W.V.S. Clothing Exchange. An appeal has been received from the Royal Devon & Exeter Hospital for help with washing up on Saturday nights. 24 members had volunteered and a rota has been formed, two members being required at a time. One Group had held a Bring and Buy Sale, realising £11 for Poppy day Funds. Many presentations had been made to Head Housewives by the various Groups.

4a. Rest Centre equipment is gradually being collected and stored. The emergency clothing bundles have now been collected from all the Centres which are closing down. These have been sorted and distributed, some to the County W.V.S., some to the Clothing Exchange, and the remainder to the Clothing Depot.

5a. The usual work has been done at the Allied Services Club, which has been very busy, and the Information Desk continues to be very popular; the visitors this month including the son of the late Mr Wendell Wilkie. Members have also been busy helping with equipment and preparing for the opening of the canteen at the new Club Room for Army Cadets.

5c. The only duty calls the Mobile Canteen had during the month were to collect equipment from a Rest Centre and several journeys for the removal of clothing from St Lawrence's Home to the Clothing Depot. CLJ459 was called in for Overseas Service, and was handed over to Region on November 30th. It is hoped to obtain another Mobile Canteen for Exeter in the near future.

6c. We still continue to help at the British Restaurant whenever required.

7a. Many of our members regularly extend hospitality to members of the Forces.

7b. Books and magazines are collected and given out to the Forces as required.

8c. Help in being given regularly in six wards at the Royal Devon & Exeter Hospital, and members also help with mending, sewing and preparing vegetables.

9. 780 knitted garments were received during the month, this number including work for the European Clothing Relief and Comforts for the Forces. We are getting a good response to the demand for knitters for the European countries, and the work is going ahead very well.

10. The usual routine work of the V.C.P. continues, and shows no signs of decreasing.

14. £184 9 6d was taken this month in Savings Stamps, which brings our Grand Total to £31,799 19 0d.

16. We continue to meet crippled trainees at the station and take them to St Loyes Training College at the request of the Ministry of Labour. One of our members is giving clerical assistance to the Secretary of the College.

17. Meetings attended this month have included the Mayor's Air Raid Distress Committee, the final Committee meeting of the Red Cross Book Drive, the final meeting of the Burton Services Club (which was destroyed during the Exeter blitz), a Salvation meeting at their Temple, the Army Cadets Council Committee meetings held by the Ministry of Fuel and Power in connection with the 'Black Diamonds' Exhibition in Exeter, and a meeting at the Shire Hall, Taunton, to discuss the School Volunteer Scheme.

18. We have met various people at the stations, and either escorted them to their destinations, or helped them to change trains. Our help was asked in connection with the Ministry of Fuel and Power Exhibition 'Black Diamonds', and we sent out many invitations and posters. Mrs McCallum and Mrs Stephens attended the opening ceremony and were afterwards entertained to tea. Mrs Goddard attended a party at the Guildhall, given by the retiring Mayoress, at which Exeter W.V.S. was cordially thanked for all the help given to the city. The Sewing Department, in addition to their usual activities, have been working on garments for the Czecho-Slovakian Relief Committee. The big excitement of the month has been the exchange of toys for Christmas, which has proved most popular, but which caused a little extra work, as only toys can be exchanged for toys. The following table of the goods handled since the opening of the exchange on May 23rd may be of interest:

articles taken in	articles given out
garments 1,688	garments 2,087
shoes 345 pairs	shoes 312 pairs

The apparent anomaly being explained by the fact that we received a number of gifts to start the Exchange.

The Whipton Orange Juice Centre is still doing very well and the members seem to really enjoy their visits.

We were able to find hospitality for one night for a W.V.S. member from Burton on Trent, and one of our members also put up a lady coming to visit her wounded son in hospital. We have had many applications for domestic helps, and also for houses or accommodation. In each case we have done the best we can, and sometimes we have been successful, but we find this question of accommodation very difficult indeed, and quite heart-rending at times. With the assistance of Region, we were able to get kitchen equipment for the Institution of the Blind purchased in London, and the Matron is very grateful. One very cold morning, an Army convoy halted outside our office, and we invited the drivers inside to have a hot drink.

Slightly to our amazement twenty-four men poured in, and our kettle worked overtime. However, the hot drinks were received with much gratitude, and apparently very much enjoyed.

The Clothing Exchange has had a very busy month, the number of 'clients' increasing all the time.[354]

December

The great winding down continued. The city watched the Home Guard march on their 'Stand Down' parade. They were congratulated by Colonel Wilsher who said 'It was fortunate indeed for all of us that their military efficiency was not put to the final test, but I am quite sure if it had been so that they would have risen to the occasion'. The Chief Constable warned men could yet be needed.[355] K. A. Goddard, County Borough Organiser for W.V.S. for Civil Defence, relaxed work hours at Christmas: she wrote 'since we can no longer say a state of emergency exists in Exeter, I propose closing this office from Friday December 22nd at 12.30 until Monday January 1st at 10 am, so as to give all the overworked voluntary office staff the proper rest they have not had for two years. The exodus of evacuee children from the South West continued with a group who had been evacuated to Cornwall arriving in Exeter en route to their own homes; they stayed overnight to break their journey. The City Librarian attempted to have the stanchions and girders removed from his muniments room; they had been placed there during the occupation of the building by the A.R.P. but were no longer needed.[356]

Some work continued: four gross of rubber teats were distributed at child welfare centres.[357] Letters continued to be sent from residents, many abroad, to the *Express & Echo* about what the rebuilt Exeter should look like. Signalman W. Shepherd of 4 Coleridge Road wrote he thought homes were the first priority and that these should be permanent and not 'shacks'. He also urged surrounding countryside should be maintained and thought High Street should be widened. The Christmas season was busy although greeting cards sold out well before Christmas Day. An exhibition at the Police Gymnasium featured toys made from wood salvaged from the blitz. Celia Johnson appeared in *This Happy Breed*, Dorothy Lamour in *The*

35. *A Christmas card sent by Captain Tom Trout, formerly a journalist with the* Express & Echo, *who noted 'what is wrong with this picture? One, no mud, two, no rain and three, Dutch girls aren't as shown, but, we do get the odd spot of off-duty'.*

Fleet's In and Esther Williams in *Bathing Beauty*. The year ended with an unusual fog, said to be the heaviest within living memory, followed by extremely icy conditions.[358]

— 1945 —

JANUARY

Cold weather continued along with a great amount of snow. Letters continued to be sent regarding individual views on reconstruction. One writer suggested women were not interested but another correspondent refuted this and pointed out she had written about it in the summer of 1942. Her view was a large underground car park was appropriate for Northernhay and questioned whether any view was being noted. Another writer thought a new plan should include deep underground shelters. A

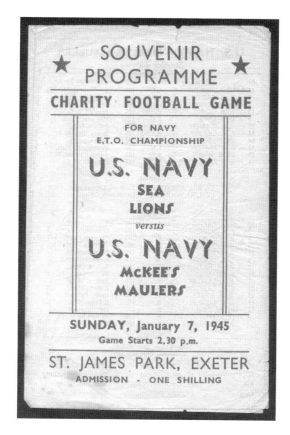

36. *Programme for a game of American football at St James Park.*

soldier stationed on the continent wrote he wanted historic buildings retained and any damaged ones repaired. He also thought High Street should be widened to end the traffic jams. Another writer thought green belts should be established in the centre another thought the city needed a good shopping arcade with a nearby nursery for mothers to leave their toddlers. He also felt housing was a priority.[359] Some reconstruction work was being finished: it was announced the first 50 of 600 temporary homes would be delivered in March. These would be erected at the St Loyes and Hamlin Lane site. At the end of the month a model was shown of the 130 permanent homes on the Wonford Estate. There was continuing debate over the Stoke Hill allotments in a dispute entitled 'Cabbages or Cottages': the city wanted the land for housing but the gardeners and the Ministry of Agriculture disagreed.

The Exeter Communist Party showed the United States Government Film *People to People*. Other entertainment included Bette Davis in *Old*

37. A plan by D. C. W. Sabine for a temporary bus station in High Street, 1 February 1945.

Acquaintance and Tom Conway in *The Falcon in Mexico*. The pantomime at the Theatre Royal, 'Jack in the Beanstalk', featured the Smarte Brothers as Jessie the Cow. Twenty-five soldiers, each injured on D Day, were guests at the Odeon and given mincemeat pies described as 'real' and like 'mother made at home'.[360]

FEBRUARY

At the Yalta Conference Churchill, Roosevelt and Stalin agreed on the plans to defeat Germany and its aftermath. Dresden was heavily bombed. In Exeter the town clerk reflected upon the setting up of air raid sirens when trying to advise another authority. He wrote 'in Exeter the contours of the city are such that sound is often completely blanketed and time and again we have had the experience that when bombs have fallen in a certain part of the city another part has heard nothing of them. For the same reason we had the greatest difficulty in locating the sirens so that they would effectively cover the whole city.'[361] He also thanked Mrs Lynwood, the Chief Housewife of the W.V.S., for the work of 'this splendid body of women' during the war. He anticipated they were 'nearly at the end of the long road when the Civil Defence Service will be able to stand down and rest from their labours'.[362] Recent thefts at the Beacon Lane Nursery Huts were solved: several juveniles were accused of stealing 36 pounds of sugar, 5 tins of evaporated milk, 6 tins of corned beef hash, 2 tins of pork and beans and a first aid box.[363] Public entertainment included Barbara Stanwyck in *Stella Dallas* and George Formby in *He Snoops To Conquer*.[364]

Opinions continued to be sent on reconstruction especially once the council discussed acquiring blitzed areas in the centre. One resident thought wider streets and modern shops resulted in better business. Brufords, the jewellers, urged that the future shape should be greatly determined by the business community but several residents pointed out all interests in the city should have a say.[365]

March

The end of the war effort in Exeter continued. The Heavitree Constitutional Club claimed substantial breakages were made while the building was used by the W.V.S. as a Rest Centre. This was disputed by the leader of the Heavitree Team; she wrote the building had been used only for a fortnight and in that time only two dinner plates had been broken. Four telephones, which had been installed at Hele's School when it was used as an Information Centre, were removed.[366] Bulldozers, mechanical grabs, fleets of lorries and a small-sized roller were seen clearing debris from the bombing and levelling areas. Goods continued to be in short supply: 'Queue up, Queue up and play the game' was said to be Exeter's slogan. Fish, cake, green groceries, ice cream, meals, the cinema and buses were among the items long lines of people were formed for.[367]

Opinions continued to be sent to the *Express & Echo* on the future Exeter. One writer urged new housing estates needed social amenities such as recreation rooms, shops, churches, schools and playing fields. The secretary of the Exeter District Gardeners' Association suggested opening up the city: in his opinion a grand crescent of buildings could be built from South Street to Southernhay and another from the Library to where Boots now stands. 'Old Exonian' urged retaining older buildings but 'Younger Generation' responded 'the sooner he builds a wall around Exeter and makes it

38. Scenes of destruction following the blitz.

39. The High Street cleared of rubble.

a museum the better'. He also wrote 'we, of the younger generation, cannot live in the past, nor can the past buy us bread and butter, if 'Old Exonian' still prefers to live in the past, let him go back to his candles, no water in houses and bad sanitation. No! We have had enough of sentimentality. It is time we cast aside the men with no foresight and put men into power with foresight'. 'Old Exonian' replied wide streets were only suitable to bring traffic into Exeter and that main shopping was better suited to narrower streets. He pointed to the experiences of other cities abroad. Another writer stressed priority should be given to building homes, especially since the armed forces were about to return. A second point was that a fitting memorial to the war should not be a cross or figures on 'cold solid granite' but a youth centre, club or a wing in the new public library.[368]

APRIL

The end of the war was in sight as Allied forces closed in on the Germans from both east and west and Hitler committed suicide in Berlin. Exeter's VE Day plans were announced on the 18th. However, President Roosevelt suddenly died and the mayor sent his condolences to the American Ambassador. One sign of the war's end was the start of dim-out, the successor to the black-out[369] and another of residents' impatience with five-hundred-gallon static water tanks in the city. These were seen as no longer necessary. It was proposed 77 of them could be broken up and removed as well as the pipe lines in the main streets.[370]

A letter was sent to city officials from Vino Sacro, the firm which supplied from Queen Street 'the perfect wine for holy communion'. It had relocated from London and was seeking the use of a public basement shelter for bonded and duty-paid cellars. The wine was used by the Admiralty and chaplains of H.M. and Allied forces. There was also a request this month from Woolworth's to remove the air raid shelter in its basement salesroom. Throughout the spring other requests were also made but there was sudden concern among officials over 'recent developments in enemy activities' in these last few weeks of the war.[371]

Letters continued to be written regarding the city's rebuilding. One resident thought all traffic should be banned from High Street except buses and tradesmen. He also thought the city needed ring roads. Before the city could be rebuilt, plans were announced for trial investigations of archaeological remains which had lain undiscovered beneath Exeter's buildings for many hundreds of years. Bombing provided an unparallel opportunity to research the past. However, criticisms were made in the press: several writers thought no useful purpose could be served by digging.[372]

40. A model for N.A.A.F.I. (the Navy, Army and Air Force Institutes) which provided canteens for servicemen throughout the country.

On St George's Day one speaker to the A.T.C. noted the Old Order had passed and stressed the 'Future holds the promise of untold wonders, of unimaginable adventures. Plunge right into them, but do so with a purpose'.[373]

May

On the 8th the end of the war against Germany was declared and crowds of people poured into the city. On the following day some 10,000 were in London Inn Square. Bells rung, there was dancing in Sidwell Street and over the next few days street parties, sports events, fancy dress parades and baby shows took place across the city. A ceremonial parade attracted large crowds but many pointed out that it did not include Americans nor members of the R.A.F., W.A.A.F., N.F.S., Civil Defence, Land Army or N.A.A.F.I. In Exeter another sign of the end of war came when staff were let go from the city's Control Centre. The Buller statue was painted white and a pair of improvised wire-framed goggles were put on the general.[374] The town clerk also announced 'the public are notified that on and after 15th

41. VE Day celebration at Bagshot Avenue.

May 1945 all public and communal shelters will be closed'. Residents were offered their Morrison shelters for one pound and one shilling or their Anderson shelters for one pound. Static water tanks, which held forty gallons, were on sale for three shillings and six pence.[375] The council's Planning Committee submitted summary notes of Thomas Sharp's plans for the rebuilding. Sharp noted it would be many months before they could be published but stressed his guiding principle was maintaining the 'intimateness of the character' of Exeter. Sharp thought wide main roads and the opening of great vistas would destroy the scale and urged now that Bedford Circus was destroyed it should be replaced with 'something which would be new and a worthy successor'.[376]

June

Public attention focused on the Far East now that Germany and Italy were defeated. Many 'raid sufferers' returned to Exeter trying to find homes and furnishings. Prisoners of War were also coming back and the city hosted small receptions. Exeter began to look more like it had once emergency water supply pipes were removed from main streets. Many residents had tripped over them during blackouts. Arrangements were made for the return of the London evacuees. There were tearful scenes at Central Station when mothers and their children bid farewell to their hosts. Some wartime arrangements continued: 603 Old Age Pensioners were served meals at

42. Programme for the Victory celebrations, 8 June 1946,
held at Heavitree.

reduced prices in the British Restaurants as well as 1,935 school dinners. Altogether there were 4,579 meals served at reduced prices which compared with 3,815 in April and 4,618 in May.[377] The Bow Sports and Fete Committee tried to obtain some portable lavatories from Exeter for free but were told they could purchase them for a reasonable rate. The toilets were just another part of the war machine being dismantled.[378]

July

The war in the pacific intensified. Double Summer Time ended on the 15th of July[379] but the extraordinary news was on the 26th with the General Election results. Exeter read the local headline 'Sensational Election Landslide to Left' but its voters gave a majority of 1,175 (16,420 to 15,245) to the Conservatives over Labour. Clement Attlee replaced Churchill and a programme of nationalization and social reform began.[380] The resumption of ordinary life continued with such events as the first of the Southern Railway's new class of engines was named after Exeter. One local journalist questioned locals as to the main topic of conversation and he discovered it was the continuation of queues. One resident reported he had purchased both fish and fruit that day; 'by nipping out in good time,' he said, 'I manage to avoid queues'. The end of the war was highlighted by the installation of new concrete streetlights in main streets. Fifty pre-fabricated shops were due to open in Sidwell Street, Paris Street, Fore Street, South Street and in Southernhay. The mayor assisted a group of a 'dozen hefty lads' in rebuilding three blitzed houses in Isca Road. Exeter was the first in the country to participate in a scheme with these apprentices. The archaeological dig in the city revealed Roman mosaics and the labour was being undertaken by six Italian collaborator prisoners of war.[381]

Public discussions continued over rebuilding. One writer questioned why new houses were being planned with a life of only ten years and another asked why the council was not placing one on public show as other councils had.[382]

AUGUST

August brought an end to hostilities in the Pacific after the dropping of atomic bombs on Hiroshima on the 6th and Nagasaki on the 9th. Immediately there were letters in the *Express & Echo* expressing shock and outrage on their use on civilian populations. Also this month there was a public meeting at the Guildhall on prisoners of war in the Far East. At the same time German Prisoners of War cleared rubble from sites in Newtown, Blackboy Road and Heavitree Road. Most of the main areas in the centre had already had debris removed. Comments were being made in the city that Exeter's 'little army' of 500 builders should be recalled from London where they had been sent. There was continued debate over rebuilding. One resident suggested the integrity of Southernhay should be preserved and questioned whether a garden of remembrance could be planned there. Another urged no construction work should take place on a Sunday but other residents responded the war did not stop on any single day and why should the war in Exeter? It was also pointed out the armed forces will be home shortly and there would be no homes for them. On the 4th 'phenomenal crowds' of 'grave elders, hopeful young couples and family parties' travelled to Rifford Road, Salter's Road and Vaughan Road in Heavitree to see the new housing. Some disparaging remarks were overheard.[383]

On the 13th plans were announced for Victory Days and on the night of the 15th rockets were set off. Two VJ Days were celebrated – VJ1 & VJ2. Besides singing and dancing in the streets there was a public bonfire on a blitzed site in Sidwell Street. Tens of thousands watched a parade which included every military contingent except the Navy – they were given the day off as a holiday. Allied flags hung over the Guildhall and Americans, French, Polish and Norwegians marched in the parade. It was said 'everyone wore the victory smile'. Street parties featured across the city including such places as Cowick Lane, Rivermead Road and Kerswill Road.[384]

Just as the VJ celebration were finishing a letter was sent to the *Express & Echo* from 'Cockney'. He, or she, wrote 'With the wonderful news of Victory it seems the appropriate time for someone to express the gratitude felt by many Londoners toward the people of Exeter. On September 1st 1939 you welcomed into your city and into your homes the children of Archbishop Sumner's Memorial School of Lambeth, and showed great kindness to us during our stay with you. I know that I speak for others as well as myself when I say that those who received us on that Friday nearly six years ago are now numbered among our greatest friends'.[385]

There was another day of celebration on the 2nd the Japanese formally surrendered. An editorial in the *Express & Echo* noted 'the struggle for victory is over, but the fight for a worth-while peace has hardly begun'.[386]

— The late 1940s —

The war was over but it took many years, in many different ways, for the home war effort to finish. One example of this was in November 1945 when the O. C. Pigeons Air Ministry awarded the Animals VC to Mary, working home pigeon of Cecil Brewer of 58 West Street, for gallantry. She had been wounded on three separate occasions and required 22 stitches. Mary had, it was said, 'delivered the goods'.[387] Another was the slow return of servicemen from abroad: one man, who had served in the RAF, came home after being imprisoned by the Japanese. There were many others. On December 11 1945 the mayor hosted a reception for survivors of HMS *Exeter* which had been sunk in the Java Sea. They had also been prisoners.[388]

The last four years of the 1940s were dominated by planning the rebuilding. Life changed in many other ways as well. For instance, in January 1947 the results of a vote on whether films should be shown on Sundays were announced: 4,310 had voted against it but 10,317 were in favour.[389]

43. *Discharge certificate of Nurse Maureen Kingsford-Lethbridge, 2 January 1946.*

POST WAR RESTRICTIONS

Restrictions continued in a number of ways including street lighting. In September 1945 the council was under instructions to cut back public street lighting: it was to be switched off at midnight except for main street junctions and other danger points. The next month summer time ended, the first time in five years.[390] In May 1946 the council was still under pressure to conserve fuel and curtail the use of street lighting. Nearly a year later, in July 1947, it sought a fifty per cent reduction on its pre-war use of lighting and intended to have full street lighting only from dusk to midnight.[391] In May 1948 the mayor wrote, with 'great reluctance', to the chairman of the lighting and cleansing department about the state of the lighting of the streets. He thought 'I am greatly disturbed at the feeling of dismay and frustration that exists among a great number of people at our darkened and totally dark streets. At one fell swoop Exeter has been thrust back into the darkest and most depressing days of the war in so far as street lighting is concerned. Not only is there dismay and depression in the minds of many, but there is also the grave risk of physical danger and injury to all who have to be abroad in our streets after dark. Broken and damaged footpaths exist all over the city, many with very little, if any, boundary to them, and the danger to life and limb, on dark nights when there is no moon will be very great. If the reason is 'economy' my only comment is that I consider the action false economy.'[392]

There were continued problems in finding clothing and in coupons. In December 1945 the council's Transport Department had difficulties extracting clothing coupons from its staff who wore civilian uniforms. It reported an additional problem with a recent burglary in which the offender was later caught but the 77 stolen clothing coupons were never recovered. In February 1947 difficulties continued. The Transport Department reported it had collected and previously forwarded 250 coupons and presented another 436 but there were 36 defaulters. It named two conductors and two conductresses for reporting to the Board of Trade. Common complaints had been 'I am sorry but my wife has all my clothing coupons' or 'I am afraid I haven't any left, you will have to wait until the next issue is made'.[393]

Food was still in short supply and gradually items were taken off rationing although it was not finally discontinued until 1954. Food arrived from unusual sources. For instance, in January 1946 a consignment arrived from the Canadian Red Cross: the butter, cheese, sardines, salt, corned beef and chocolate bars were given to the poor.[394] Shortly afterwards, in April, a letter was sent to the Mayor from Mr W. E. Thompson of New South Wales regarding a parcel of food for an Exeter family. He wanted to express his gratitude for refreshments given to him in 1916 when travelling through the city on a troop train from Devonport to Tidworth. In May 1946 the council tried to increase supplies of tea by transferring ownership of a stock it had purchased four years earlier for the war effort. It suggested the tea would deteriorate if not consumed.[395]

44. Food rationing book, 1952-3.

CIVIL DEFENCE

Slowly civil defence was dismantled. In November 1945 the organiser for the W.V.S. attempted to stand down. Regional office told her the group must stay in full operation even though the staff felt their services were no longer needed. However, the Exeter women replied 'we have all got very weary, and we have a lot of other work to do, and we also feel very strongly that we joined on definitely for War Service and not for post-war social service.'[396] Work continued. In March 1946 the W.V.S. reported 'the chief activity this month has been moving the office from Paul Street to our clothing depot on St David's Hill. It was a terrific job. All papers, circulars and letters had to be looked through and the out of date ones destroyed. The amount of salvage collected was stupendous. All furniture, except two tables, the filing cabinet and one electric stove were handed back to the city, and all borrowed furniture returned to the owners.

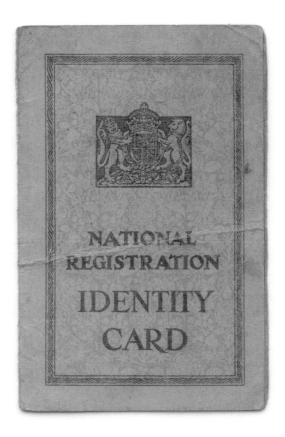

45. *National Identity Card, 1949. These lasted through the 1940s.*

Apart from that our chief activities were keeping an eye on the Dutch children staying in the city and helping the Foster Mothers with clothes, food, etc., also helping with entertainments for them, assisting the Mayor with the distribution of some wonderful cases of gift foods from the people of Australia to all the families on Poor Law Relief in the City, and, as usual, helping with Air Raid Distress Relief cases. The YMCA had to close their Hostel for Service girls, but were lucky in finding a new place, and some members have been helping them get it started and assist in the Canteens in the afternoons. Members are doing this in their private capacity and not as W.V.S. Several members continue to help at the A.C. and Whipton Welfare Food Centre has been busy. The Knitting Department had finally closed having dispatched all the remaining socks to the Devon Regt. Comforts, and 46 garments to E. Relief. Clothing Department has been busy packing and dispatching all the second hand clothes. The National Savings Dept. collected stamps £92 19s, certificates £141 15s, bonds £15, making a total for the month of £249 14s and a grand total to date of £40,488 13s 6d. The clothing exchange has been fairly busy taking in [blank number of] garments and [blank] pairs of shoes, and giving out [blank] garments and [blank] shoes. It is hoped to keep a few private knitting circles going in our own homes. We have such excellent knitters in Exeter I would be a pity to let it drop while there is still a need.'[397]

Civil defence installations were removed throughout the late 1940s. For instance, in December 1945 plans were made to remove the observation post on Constitutional Hill. It was established in 1940 along with two others at Ludwell Lane in Wonford and at the Fire Headquarters at Danes Castle. Special constables manned the first two and sent either 'hot' news (reports at the time of sightings) or 'cold' news (reports made in the following morning).[398] In January 1946 the peacetime use of shelters was discussed. Applications were made to the War Emergency Committee to use one at the Triangle by the police, for the Livery Dole shelter to be used for storage by the council, that at Whipton By-pass as a workshop and the one at Isca Road for industrial use. In October 1946 four shelters on private land near the railway line were demolished. This was just part of a general scheme to clear them.[399] Most staff was let go before the end of the war and in September 1946 a reunion was suggested of the Industrial Civil Defence Liaison Committee which coordinated various A.R.P. services and industry but the town clerk wrote 'quite frankly I do not think it would justify the trouble involved'. Less than a year later, in June 1947, the A.R.P. office at Heavitree House finally closed down.[400]

The end of the war brought new dangers. In September 1946 the Mayor had received a certificate for the two beds given by Exeter to City Clinical Hospital in Stalingrad which had been a token of their admiration of the heroic stand made against the Germans. But one year later, in September 1947, the council appointed Major A. Lock as Civil Defence Officer (part-time) who promptly arranged two lectures on 'Civil Defence in the Future' and 'The Atomic Bomb'. He had been Deputy A.R.P. Controller during the war.[401] In December the Chief Constable and his staff were invited to a lantern and cinema lecture at the Guildhall on 'problems created by atomic attacks and the lessons to be drawn there from for application to our own post war plans' and 'the more important effects of bombing raids upon the Japanese people and their homes'. The lectures were arranged 'in view of the possible return to life of the civil defence services'. In March 1947 the Home Office had informed the council local authorities to keep sirens in case they were needed again.[402] The Cold War had begun.

— Part Two —

Post War Reconstruction, 1945 to 1949

The last four years of the 1940s saw the pace of the discussions and events described in the previous pages intensity. The city was consumed by planning reconstruction.

The extent of the loss was colossal: one secret report, completed on 10 May 1942, concluded the main shopping centre was 'wiped out'.[403] Another on the same date, by a member of the fire service, initially listed 620 buildings damaged and 550 destroyed[404] but by the end of the war the number increased to some 17,000 damaged and 1,800 destroyed.[405] How to rebuild these houses and other buildings took more than twenty years to decide and achieve. Much public criticism has been made of the decisions particularly of the destruction of historic buildings after the bombing but also in the reconstruction plans. It is no coincidence that the only written studies were made by John Brierley, City Engineer and Surveyor from 1948 to 1972, and Norman Venning, who was in the City Engineer's Department from 1945 to 1974. Both men were closely involved in it and not surprisingly their accounts justify the manner of redevelopment.[406]

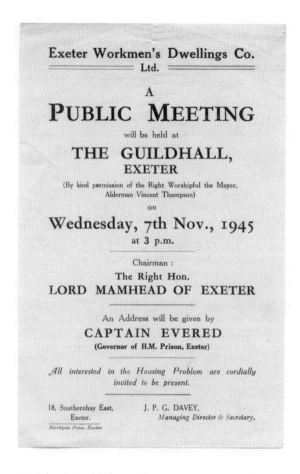

46. Advertising bill for public meeting regarding housing,
7 November 1945.

HISTORIC BUILDINGS

In 1942 the city had experienced three hundred years of peace. The last period of destruction from war happened in the 1640s and most of that involved buildings outside the city walls. The previous time in which the centre may have been so heavily damaged could have been when the Vikings attacked in 876 and 1003.[407] Over the centuries continual changes were made, notably following the outbreak of cholera in 1832, but most of these were done on a piecemeal basis. Fire was not as great a threat as it was in other Devon places and many changes came through commercial redevelopment. One building generally replaced another. In 1942 Exeter was a city filled with a mix of building styles and many of them were ancient.[408]

Immediately after the blitz the town clerk began demolishing important buildings which were damaged. As seen above, Newman ordered the remains of Bedford Circus to be destroyed even though some owners tried to save their individual properties. He also had the Commercial Union building demolished despite attempts to save it by the ministry in charge of ancient properties. Newman's request for explosives to destroy buildings may have been one of necessity but it is interesting to ponder which buildings he had in mind. He was refused the explosives but he might have acquired them from other means, possibly from the military. Newman was clearly deceptive and dishonest in correspondence regarding Bedford Chapel. Presumably he perceived commercial advantages in having a landscape free of impediments to redevelopment to be overwhelmingly necessary. Newman appears to have wanted a modern Exeter or at least one in the centre. This was his argument regarding the Saxon fragment of St George's church found along South Street. It was suggested to him the stonework should be preserved but Newman regarded this as an unwanted and unnecessary obstacle to his rebuilding plans. The council had not been unconcerned with its ancient buildings. For instance, in recent memory it had invested in St Nicholas Priory, two houses on Stepcote Hill and the Chevalier House on Fore Street. However, the blitz had, unfortunately, offered commercial opportunities which overrode heritage considerations.

Newman's own file of correspondence regarding historic buildings is revealing. The collection was deposited in the archives after he retired and it is interesting to ponder whether Newman would have agreed such damning material should have been lodged for posterity. Much of the file concerns negotiations with Mr B. H. St John O'Neil, Inspector of Ancient Monuments. He came to Exeter on May 16 to assess which historic buildings should be saved. O'Neil worked in the Ministry of Works and Buildings and was quickly in dispute with city officials. On 26 May he provided a list of 23 buildings to be preserved until there was sufficient time to consider their merits. Some he admitted could be recorded and then later demolished. The Inspector tried to be helpful in suggesting government grants would be forthcoming in some instances and reported he and his team would arrange temporary work to make the buildings safe. Included among these were Numbers 15 to 20 Bedford Circus[409] but unfortunately on 9 June O'Neil was informed of their collapse. O'Neil responded he was 'exceedingly surprised' to hear this news. He had already agreed the rest of Bedford Circus was regarded as a 'total loss' and that he was not willing to allow the city to demolish the remains. On the first of July he refused permission but Exeter's officials wanted to demolish the buildings and reopen the road to traffic. They even claimed to be ignorant of the original shape of the circus and O'Neil suggested they looked at photographs in a particular book which showed Bedford Circus before the blitz. He also informed the city the remains should be incorporated in the new development plan. The Inspector prevailed in the short term but by the end of September Newman had a letter from the city's chief constable supporting him that the buildings impeded traffic. O'Neil still insisted on preservation. On 26 January the city informed the Inspector they had declared the buildings unsafe and would demolish them. They succeeded.

This was one particular area in which city authorities showed a disregard for older buildings. There were some points on which the two parties seemed to agree: the inspector wrote he was grateful for their work to preserve ancient timber from 166 Fore Street, agreed Norman House and St John's Hospital could be demolished and expressed his thanks for work on the churches of St Stephen and St Mary Arches. But there were also grave problems brought out in O'Neil's July report. He requested parts of both Dix's Field and Southernhay East should be kept and asked that an unspecified building in Fore Street, Beargate in South Street and the façade of the Commercial Union Assurance Company building be saved. The inspector also wanted the Saxon remains at the church of St George kept but, as seen in the pages above, the town clerk was vehemently against this. The city authorities were not happy with all of these requests, particularly with the Commercial Union building which was subsequently destroyed. The two parties had already met about Bampfylde House and the ministry reluctantly agreed to defer decisions on saving it, mainly because of the shortage of labour.

The inspector was most distressed by the city's involvement in two particular buildings. In early July a colleague of the inspector had found contractors pulling down part of the almshouse in Catherine Street despite the city agreeing it would be saved. The inspector wrote 'it is indeed fortunate that he was there at the right time'. The most damning example involved Black Lions Inn on South Street, a building formerly owned by the Priory of Plympton. The inspector's comments on the city's actions are extraordinary. O'Neil reported great damage had been done by a demolition gang after his visit on 20 May; the men had pulled down a medieval window with a rope and a medieval wall was removed. This caused the inspector to write:

As you may have gathered, I prefer speaking my mind in certain cases rather than nursing a grievance, and I can say definitely that in my experience this is the worst case of vandalism which I have known to be perpetuated after a raid anywhere in England under the aegis of a local authority. I put it thus strongly because before the demolition there was preserved almost intact two sides of a major feature of medieval Exeter. No one can yet tell me what it was, but clearly there was a large Hall of normal type, perhaps of a guild.

Two aspects of the matter make it especially galling. One is that the city of Exeter prides itself upon its ancient buildings, and attracts visitors to them as much as it can. The other is that our Salvage Scheme, as we call it, for Historic Buildings is intended to deal with just such a situation. The City Architect being unable to act for us, as we had hoped, we did the work ourselves, and made this building one of our special cases both in your office verbally on May 22nd and later in my letter to you of May 26th.

There will be no point in holding a 'post-mortem' examination, since that will not replace the vanished walling. It may well be that things did not go quite as you yourself wished, and that there were 'extenuating circumstances'. I would, however, ask two things. The first is that what still remains of the building is not touched by the gangs, so that later we can do the necessary work to make it secure for the time being. The other point is that I hope you really will make certain in other cases, such as the Church Army House, and Country House Inn [in Catherine Street], that there can be no recurrence of this regrettable happening.'[410]

Few of the buildings were actually preserved by the city. A year and a half later there was another dispute over Bedford Chapel. The decision on its future was delayed until the end of November 1943 when it was once again raised. The inspector had agreed with the bishop that the chapel would be retained. However, the town clerk questioned whether the building was historic and, with great deception, added that this was 'quite news to me'.[411] As noted above on page 87, the clerk neglected to acknowledge he was in office during the campaign to save the chapel by the Society for the Protection of Ancient Buildings. The building was subsequently demolished.

THOMAS SHARP'S PLAN

After months of discussion the council began planning rebuilding. In October 1943 Plymouth published its great scheme[412] and that month Thomas Sharp, a town planner and President of the Town Planning Institute, was employed by Exeter as consultant. He submitted summary points in May 1945, on 28 December the plan was on show at the library and in March 1946 it was published as *Exeter Phœnix, a plan for rebuilding by Thomas Sharp*. That month the council accepted his plan in broad outline.[413] His scheme involved a 'freeway', an inner-by pass, to the immediate north of the city (running from Blackboy Road to New North Road via a tunnel under Northernhay) and another which would have linked Exe Bridge with Magdalen Street

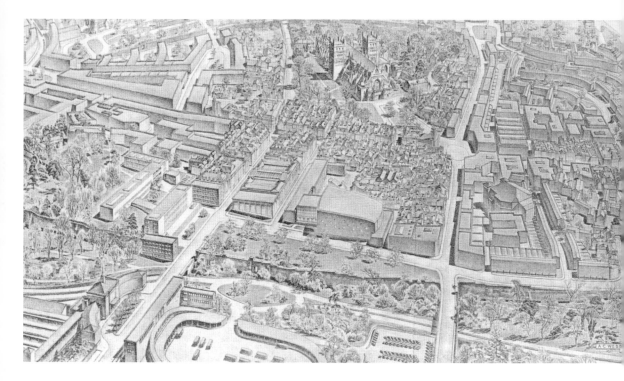

47. A new Exeter. It is difficult to identify modern Exeter with Sharp's vision. This view is taken from Queen Street looking south. Sharp wanted Rougemont Hotel replaced by a bus station, the museum rebuilt ('an architectural horror'), Bradninch Place below Rougemont Castle demolished, a new hall created on Paul Street (where the Guildhall Shopping Centre is now) and the creation of what later became Princesshay.

and Holloway Street. He also planned a wider High Street with roundabouts at either end of High Street. That at the junction of High and Sidwell Streets would have been approximately as large in its ground space as the cathedral and similar to schemes at Plymouth. Finally, he planned the creation of the pedestrian shopping centre which became Princesshay.

Sharp's plan is interesting in its detail. For instance, he deplored the building of the Odeon which he felt towered over the landscape on Sidwell Street. It was, he wrote, 'a shapeless lump of a building which rides the city like a totalitarian mammonite cathedral'. He felt strongly that the style of architecture should be modern and was contemptuous of rebuilding it in its old form: restoration was undesirable and sympathetic not ruthless renewal was the watchword.[414] At the unveiling Sharp asked what kind of city should there be? The *Express & Echo* thought a public poll would

48. *Sharp's view from St Thomas shows a new traffic system leading into Fore Street. An inner bypass to the south of the walls linked with South Street which would be entirely rebuilt except for a stretch from the Catholic church to Palace Gate. The White Hart and George's Meeting Hall would have been demolished. The Carfax (the corner of High, Fore, South and North Streets) was to be rebuilt with all surrounding buildings destroyed. Only a portion of the centre would have had buildings constructed earlier than 1945.*

support retaining the old character rather than a revolution in reconstruction. The exhibition drew large crowds and general opinion was said to be 'very nice but we shan't live to see it'.[415] The plan was not completely followed for a number of reasons.

Rebuilding

In October 1948 the council passed a three-year plan for rebuilding: £1,100,000 was earmarked to build Princesshay, token rebuilding in Sidwell and South Streets and for some work in High Street.[416] Actual work began three months later, in January 1949, some six years and eight months after the blitz. In 1980 John Brierley, who began as City Engineer and Surveyor

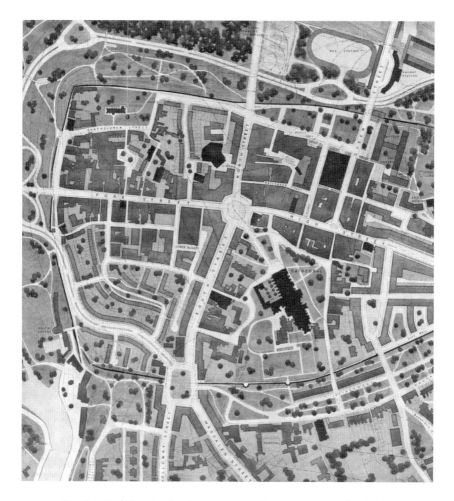

49. Detail of Sharp's plan for a new roundabout at the Carfax, 1945.

in 1948, listed reasons for the delay. First, a number of senior appointments had to be made including his own. Second, Brierley felt Sharp's plan was idealistic but not practical and it did not fit Exeter's needs. Moreover, in his view Sharp exceeded his remit by providing a detailed report when only an outline plan had been asked for. The outcome, according to Brierley, was the council pulled Sharp's plan 'to pieces'. There were other reasons. Traders were keen to open in new premises but landowners were reluctant to allow temporary buildings and the first building licences were not issued until five years went by. There were also problems with new ground rents and with developers. He felt local residents wanted a traditional style of architecture and the council was unable to fully accept modern styles. Growing commercial pressures forced the council to concentrate more on the progress

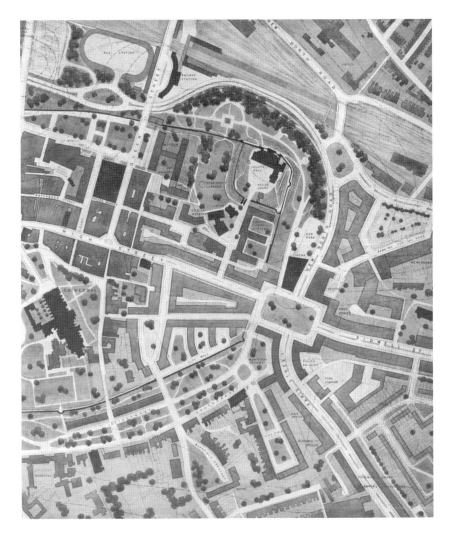

50. Sharp planned a new square at the meeting point of High and
Sidwell Streets, 1945.

of rebuilding with the consequence that architectural style took second
place. Brierley felt there was a compromise in building styles in the early
years and that this was due to the public longing for the old and its reluctance
to accept the new. In his view the first buildings with quality modern designs
came later with the Post Office, Public Library and Guildhall Shopping
Centre. He wrote in 1980 that gradually the older generation, with its
unrealistic nostalgia for the past, was being replaced by a younger one.
He felt the architectural taste of Exeter was improving.[417]

The rebuilding process was complicated in that it involved adapting an

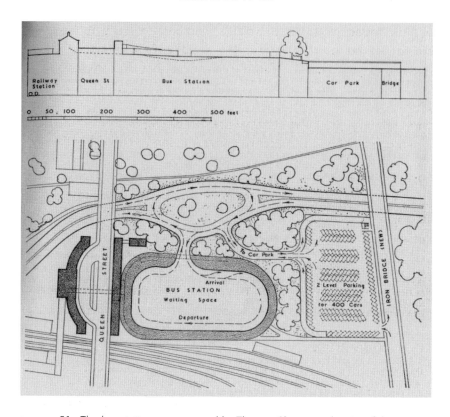

51. The bus station, as proposed by Thomas Sharp, on the site of the
Rougemont Hotel, 1945.

ancient city to modern needs and planning new streets, retail premises and
estates for housing and light industry. Sharp's northern bypass was rejected
but another running along the southern walls, known as Western Way, was
begun in 1954 and finished, in sections, in 1964. In 1949 the council
agreed this bypass, planned by Brierley, and allocated £815,000 for it.
Sharp's northern plan was estimated to cost £2,118,000. In 1969 and
1972 two new bridges over the Exe were added to Sharp's plan which
increased the effectiveness of the bypass. Other street changes involved
widening Fore Street and Sidwell Street in the early 1950s. Service roads
were created from adjacent older roads including George Street. Cowick
Street was also widened following the construction of the new bridges.[418]
The most startling changes were in housing and retail.

Housing

Through the war there was continued public pressure to replace housing.

The city hosted thousands of evacuees and had lost many homes. It was recognised that once the war was finished there would not be enough housing to accommodate returning men and women. The city immediately began to repair homes but by August 1947 there were still 3,303 houses with war damage. Twenty-nine had been repaired during that month and another twenty-three were in the process of being worked on.[419] There was a shortage of labour, and as seen above, the sending of 500 of the city's labourers to London was bitterly resented.

More than 600 temporary houses were being planned, including in Hamlin Lane, in January 1945 but there were considerable delays. In the summer of 1945 permanent housing was built in Rifford Road, Salter's Road and Vaughan Road and this created great excitement. Temporary homes were still being built in 1948 and in 1949 new roads were constructed. In 1949 Princess Elizabeth opened Toronto House, the home for the elderly. This was part of the sixty-acre site at Stoke Hill. In 1951 another council housing estate was established at Countess Wear (100 acres) and there was a further 100 acres at Whipton Barton North and Whipton Barton South. Work continued through the 1950s and into the early 1960s on these estates as well as others.[420]

These houses are still standing and have made homes for several generations. They are unlikely to be demolished. It is the nature of home-owning in the early twenty-first century that residential buildings are improved but not destroyed to make way for new buildings. That tends to be the unfortunate fate of commercial buildings which are at the whim of developers.

COMMERCIAL PROPERTIES

The shortage of retail space was immediately apparent after the blitz. Through the 1940s there was a desperate need from both firms and individuals. For instance, in October 1947 Francis Skeet, who designed stained glass, tried to find studio accommodation to replace that lost in Bedford Circus including his 500 books, papers, cartoons, photographs and artists' materials. His residence at 4 Pennsylvania Park was untouched. The city centre was cleared of debris, partly by prison labour,[421] and signs erected on empty lots indicated where shops had stood and where they might be relocated. These were in place through the 1940s. Clearance work included more than just clearing rubble. Several churchyards had graves exhumed and remains reburied; St Lawrence's Church on High Street had 365 graves dealt with and there were other sites, including St

George's church in South Street, which also needed to be cleared. During the winter of 1946/7 temporary shops were erected at the top of Southernhay near the East Gate and on the site of the Lower Market on Fore Street (now George's Market). While these were being built the city set about acquiring areas blitzed in the centre by compulsory purchase. By 1945 the Exeter Blitzed Traders' Association formed and became very vocal in their lobbying for rebuilding, a public inquiry on the plans was held at the Guildhall in December 1945 and in spite of considerable opposition from existing retailers the council was granted the powers in September 1947.[422]

The actual rebuilding began on 8 January 1949 for Bedford Street but it took much longer for buildings to follow.[423] On 21 October 1949 Princess Elizabeth came to Exeter and marked the rebuilding by unveiling a plaque for the new pedestrian shopping centre. The street had yet to be built and the ceremony took place at the ornamental feature which stood within a vast waste ground. Shortly afterwards the Mayor received a letter from the princess' household that 'she was very glad to have the opportunity of taking part in the ceremony of fixing in position the tablet marking the beginning of the rebuilding of the centre of the city . . . Her Royal Highness thought the luncheon quite excellent and was greatly impressed by the beauty of your ancient guildhall'. In 1950 work began on Princesshay and

52. *Princess Elizabeth at Exeter, October 1949.*

it finished 12 years later.[424] Meanwhile, other efforts were being made to increase retail space. In 1948 the council acquired 48 acres in Marsh Barton and this formed the basis for the large estate.

The majority of Exeter's rebuilding work happened in the 1950s and 1960s. After Bedford Street was started in 1949 the car park at Mary Arches Street was opened and then Bystock Green. Slowly other parts of the city were rebuilt. The programme included streets, sewers, housing estates and commercial premises. High Street itself was not built until the 1950s and there was a shortage of housing for many years after the war.

It is interesting that at the time in which this book has been completed Princesshay is about to be redeveloped. It is said a building stands the greatest chance of being demolished once it reaches 50 years old and when it is not yet 100. Across England many buildings from the immediate post-war era are currently being taken down. They are unfashionable: perceived as unresponsive to modern needs and poorly and crassly-built in a period in which austerity ruled. In 1980 Brierley judged Princesshay as having been an 'architectural compromise'. Yet, it now has supporters and Exeter has seen a very vocal campaign to keep Princesshay. It is ironic that for many years it was derided because it was built on the ruins of Bedford Circus, widely acknowledged as the city's best example of Georgian architecture. Now, half a century later, Princesshay itself is seen as historic and worth saving. It is praised as the country's first pedestrian shopping centre and yet has been sharply observed as being pedestrian in both meanings of the word.[425] Another of the main arguments for keeping Princesshay rests on the assumption modern architecture will inevitably be poorer.

Public opinion on rebuilding was expressed through the 1940s in the letter pages of the *Express & Echo*. In August 1944 one serviceman, describing himself as being banished for five years, wrote 'are we to return to an Exeter hampered, as in the past, by narrow streets, appalling traffic blocks & the dull, depressing type of architecture so favoured by certain stick-in-the-muds?' He strongly felt Exeter should not be a garden city with open views and excessively wide streets but a 'sane and orderly city'. His closing thoughts were that he, and many other military men, would return to 'a brave new world' and wanted 'a brave new Exeter'.[426] It is important to remember some residents thought modern buildings were a mark of progress.

What is also interesting is how Princesshay managed to be built. City authorities viewed particular ancient buildings in the same way some plants are considered to be weeds: they were in the wrong place. Despite continued public requests for Bedford Circus to be rebuilt there was no apparent support amongst the local authorities. Any opposition had little or no effect. Exeter did not have its civic society until the early 1960s, nearly one hundred and fifty years later than the first one in Devon.[427] In the 1940s there was no effective opposition nor did local government want to preserve. Instead, the aim was to create a new Exeter, similar to how Plymouth was built. In some ways this was the way of the future; sixty years later modern retail outlets do not have distinctive features in the way that, for instance, the Bruford's building was constructed, but are large, characterless units set in a jumble away from town centres. They aspire to be like a modern American town with no centre or high street, merely scattered shopping malls along highways with ample parking. Newman and his officials were no doubt envious of their Plymouth counterparts: their centre was almost entirely destroyed by the Germans and they were able to rebuild on a scale Exeter could not hope to achieve. Exeter's officials had to remove medieval obstacles the Germans had not destroyed and only then were they able to plan in their entirety the developments of Bedford Precinct, Princesshay and High Street as well as South and Sidwell Streets. Princesshay is a symbol of that determination.

In 1946 Alderman Tarr, then Mayor, said Hitler had compelled them to deal with some of the city's worst features and felt that old and new would easily stand together in a rebuilt Exeter. Moreover, it would, he thought, represent the ideals and aspirations of the city.[428] Sixty years later it could be reasonably argued that the city's record in building homes was exemplary but the decisions made in rebuilding the centre remain contentious.

— Conclusion —

The 1940s were years of war, destruction and rebirth. The most visible mark on Exeter is in the landscape. This loss of older buildings and the rebuilding of new ones symbolises other changes: the war took the lives of many local people who were fighting overseas or at home in the war effort. The gaps are there but as time goes by they become less apparent and their places are filled by new arrivals.

Some individuals made tremendous efforts after the bombings and it is a pity we have not collectively remembered them. The city should also be proud of its war contribution in hosting thousands of evacuees. No doubt many young lives were saved because of it. Each year there are fewer of the generation that lived through this decade and not many today can appreciate the demands made in daily economies and, moreover, personal sacrifices. Invasion was a constant threat and it is unimaginable now to think of the Nazis occupying the city. Fortunately it did not happen. It would be unrealistic to expect Exeter will never experience war again but hopefully it will be many years in the future before such death and destruction will be known again.

The 1940s were also a story of rebirth, of a generation trying to build a better Exeter. Lessons should have been learned: the reconstruction was a project unparalleled in the city's recorded history and which overwhelmed it for nearly a generation. It will be interesting to see whether modern society, in its planning and development, has learned to better assess Exeter's needs and able to meet whatever new opportunities arise in the future.

53. The award given to Tom Pike, fire watcher at the Co-operative building at the corner of Paris and High Street on the night of the blitz. Adjacent buildings were destroyed by fire but Mr Pike and three other men fought the flames and saved their building. Each was recognised by the Exeter Wholesale Co-operative Society with a gold watch and certificate. A photograph of Mr Pike is also included on the bottom-right side.

Illustration Sources

Permission to publish illustrations has been given by Polestar Wheatons Ltd (Illustrations 1, 2, 5, 11, 23, 27, 39); *Express & Echo* (6–7, 9, 12, 24–6, 30, 33–5, 37–8, 52); Exeter City Council (4, 8, 14, 28–9, 31, 40, 47–51); anonymous private collections (3, 17–22, 32); private collection of Dick Passmore (10, 13, 16, 36, 41–6); private collection of Graham Parnell (15) and private collection of Maurice Pike (53). Copyright rests with the holders.

— Notes —

1. Devon Record Office (hereafter DRO), 70/12. It was written in 1942 and deposited at the city record office in 1970, by which time Whiteside had lost the final page.

2. The exception is a general series of memories published by the Fountain Community Association in the 1970s: *People Talking* edited by Jenny Lloyd, nine vols.

3. The book is also incomplete because it is not possible to include some of the social details which appeared in the *Express & Echo*. Much of this information was morale-raising such as, for example, fundraising efforts and social events.

4. Todd Gray, *Lost Exeter: Five Centuries of Change* (Exeter, 2002); Todd Gray (ed.), *Exeter: The Travellers' Tales* (Exeter, 2000), 182–3, 171.

5. W. G. Hoskins, *Two Thousand Years in Exeter* (Exeter, 1960), 130–1.

6. DRO, ECA/town clerk's papers (hereafter TC), group o, box 19/air raid precautions book.

7. *Express & Echo* (hereafter E&E), 21 Dec. 1973 and 26 July 1961.

8. *The Story of the Exeter Blitz* (Exeter, 1942); *This Jewel Remains: the record of the German Baedeker Raid on Exeter, the cathedral capital of the west, on May 4th, 1942.* (no place of publication or date given); D. P. Davies, *The Bombing of Exeter* (Exeter, 1973); Geoff Worrall, *Target Exeter* (Exeter, 1979); Peter Thomas, *Fire on the Wind* (Exeter, 1992, reprinted as *Exeter Burning*).

9. John Brierley, 'Exeter, 1939–74: The reconstruction of a city' (MA thesis, University of Manchester, 1980); Norman Venning, ts at Westcountry Studies Library entitled 'The Reconstruction of the Central Areas of Exeter, 1945–1965', 1977, published as *Exeter, the blitz and rebirth of the city* (Exeter, 1988).

10. TC, group o, box 22/88.

11. TC, group o, box 29/2.

12. DRO, ECA, Engineer's and Surveyor's Papers, box 76.

13. DRO, ECA, Engineer's and Surveyor's Papers, box 76.

14. DRO, 70/12.

15. TC, group o, box 25/301.

16. DRO, 70/12.

17. DRO, 32792/Z1.

18. Worrall, *Target Exeter*, 6.

19. E&E, 18 Dec. 1944.

20. Norman Longmate, *How we lived then* (1971), 229.

21. TC, group j, box 8/135.

22. TC, group j, box 8/135.

23. *The Daily Mail*, 23 May 1942; TC, group o, box 25/307.

24. TC, group j, box 9/147.

25. TC, group j, box 7/'number of evacuated blind lists'; group j, box 9/142; group j, box 9/146; group j, box 8/138; group j, box 9/146.

26. TC, group j, box 8/137.

27. E&E 12 June 1943.

28. E&E, 27 Sept. 1939.

29. E&E, 1–9, 23 Sept. 1939.

30. E&E, 14 Sept. 1939.

31. E&E, 11 & 16 Sept. 1939.

32. E&E, 16 Sept. 1939; Longmate, *How we lived*, 216.

33. E&E, 27, 29–30 Sept. 1939.

34. TC, group o, box 18/212; E&E, 16 Sept. 1939.

35. E&E, 27 Sept. 1939.

36. Longmate, *How we lived*, 228.

37. E&E, 7, 11, 17 & 25 Oct. 1939, 27 Sept. 1939.

38. TC, group N, box 10; E&E, 4, 11, 18, 22, 29 Nov. 1939. Brittain died in 1970. Her daughter is Shirley Williams, one of the founders of the Social Democrats: DNB.

39. E&E, 2, 4 & 9 Dec. 1939.

40. TC, group o, box 15/174.

41. E&E, 9, 27 & 30 Dec. 1939.

42. Longmate, *How we lived*, 287.

43. E&E, Jan. 1940.

44. TC, group n, box 10.

45. TC, group l, box 3/35.

46. TC, group o, box 21/256.

47. Longmate, *How we lived*, 99.

48. *The Western Times*, 23 Feb. 1940.

49. E&E, 16 & 17 Feb. 1940; Longmate, *How we lived*, 47.

50. TC, group l, box 18/202.

51. E&E, 23 & 24 Feb. 1940.

52. E&E, 24 Feb. 1940.

53. *The Western Times*, 1 March 1940.

54. Longmate, *How we lived*, 141.

55. E&E, 7 March 1940; DRO, ECA/1/61, report 19 March 1940; DRO, ECA/11/2, Allotments Comm. report, 25 April 1940; *The Western Times*, 15 March 1940.

56. DRO, ECA/1/61, report 23 April 1940.

57. TC, group n, box 14.

58. TC, group n, box 12.

59. TC, group o, box 20/234.

60. E&E, 14 & 9 March 1940.

61. Longmate, *How we lived*, 104.

62. TC, group l, box 18/202.

63. DRO, ECA/1/61, report 28 May 1940; TC, group o, box 15/174.

64. TC, group o, box 16/181.

65. TC, group o, box 15/ARP circulars, Jan. – May 1940; TC, group o, box 19/230; TC, group n, box 14.

66. TC, group n, box 11/111; TC, group n, box 14/113.

67. TC, group o, box 15/174; TC, group o, box 17/197.

68. TC, group o, box 20/240.

69. TC, group o, box 20/245; WMN, 12 June 1940. Another Italian taken was Fungo Morelli, who had an ice cream business in Summerland Street: Jenny Lloyd (ed.), *People Talking* (Exeter, 1977), VII, 32.

70. Longmate, *How we lived*, 141, 281.

71. TC, group n, box 14/153.

72. TC, group n, box 10; DRO, ECA/1/61, report 23 July 1940; TC, group o, box 20/ no reference.

73. TC, group o, box 20/233.

74. TC, group m, box 7.

75. TC, group m, box 7/71.

76. TC, group o, box 19/221; TC, group o, box 21/256.

77. TC, group o, box 16/184.

78. TC, group o, box 21/260.

79. Davies, *Bombing*, introduction.

80. TC, group o, box 20/235.

81. TC, group o, box 19/230.

82. TC, group o, box 20/235. 8 windows had damage: DRO, 3004A/PZ78.

83. TC, group o, box 19/230.

84. TC, group o, box 17/187.

85. TC, group o, box 20/no reference.

86. TC, group o, box 20/no reference.

87. TC, group o, box 17/187.

88. TC, group o, box 18/212.

89. TC, group o, box 15/174.

90. TC, group o, box 19/221.

91. TC, group n, box 11/116.

92. TC, group o, box 20/235.

93. TC, group o, box 19/230.

94. TC, group o, box 19/221; TC, group o, box 17/187; TC, group o, box 18/207.

95. DRO, ECA/1/61, report 24 Sept. 1940.

96. TC, group n, box 14.

97. TC, group n, box 14.

98. DRO, ECA/1/61, report 22 October 1940.

99. TC, group o, box 29/371.

100. TC, group o, box 18/202.

101. TC, group n, box 14.

102. TC, group n, box 14.

103. TC, group j, box 7/131 & 9/146.

104. TC, group o, box 20/235 & 19/230. See also Janet and Steve Bowen (ed.), *Millennium Project 2000: Wonford* (Wonford, 2000), 5.

105. TC, group o, box 18/198.

106. TC, group o, box 19/230.

107. TC, group o, box 20/241; TC, group o, box 18/202.

108. DRO, ECA/1/61, report 29 Nov. 1940; TC, group n, box 14.

109. TC, group l, box 3/34; TC, group o, box 18/198.

110. TC, group o, box 16/181.

111. TC, group o, box 19/230.

112. TC, group o, box 20/235; TC, group o, box 18/207.

113. E&E, 1 & 17 Jan. 1941.

114. TC, group n, box 14; TC, group o, box 17/188.

115. E&E, 4, 7 & 8 Jan. 1941; Longmate, *How we lived*, 135.

116. DRO, ECA/1/62, report 28 Jan. 1941; E&E, 9 Jan. 1941.

117. DRO, ECA/1/62, report 17 Sept. 1941; TC, group l, box 3/31.

118. E&E, 1 Jan. 1941.

119. E&E, 3, 23 & 25 Jan. 1941.

120. TC, group o, box 19/230; E&E 17 Jan. 1941.

121. DRO, ECA/1/62, report 25 Feb. 1941, ECA/11/2, Allotments Comm. report, 3 Feb. 1941.

122. E&E, 1 Feb. 1941; TC, group o, box 19/ 230; E&E, 24 Jan. & 21 Feb. 1941.

123. TC, group o, box 19/230; E&E, 1 Feb. 1941.

124. TC, group n, box 12/127.

125. E&E, 1 March 1941.

126. Longmate, *How we lived*, 141.

127. TC, group o, box 20/no reference; TC, group o, box 19/229.

128. TC, group o, box 19/230; TC, group o, box 22/282.

129. TC, group o, box 18/207.

130. TC, group o, box 21/260; Longmate, *How we lived*, 130.

131. TC, group o, box 22/88.

132. TC, group o, box 17/187.

133. E&E, 9 April 1941.
134. DRO, ECA/11/2, Allotments Comm. report, 8 April 1941; TC, group k, box 2.
135. TC, group k, box 2/25.
136. TC, group o/box 17/197.
137. TC, group n, box 14; E&E 19 & 7 April 1941; TC, group o, box 20/no reference.
138. Longmate, *How we lived*, 141.
139. DRO, ECA/11/2, Allotments Comm. report, 19 May 1941.
140. TC, group k, box 2.
141. TC, group o, box 22/279.
142. TC, group o, box 23/290.
143. TC, group o, box 18/207.
144. TC, group o, box 22/282.
145. TC, group o, box 16/184.
146. TC, group o, box 22/263.
147. TC, group n, box 10; E&E, 6 May 1941.
148. TC, group o, box 23/290.
149. TC, group o, box 22/264.
150. E&E, 28 June 1941.
151. TC, group o, box 17/188.
152. TC, group o, box 23/290.
153. Bowen, *Wonford*, 6.
154. E&E, 28 June 1941.
155. TC, group o, box 22/271.
156. TC, group o, box 17/197.
157. TC, group o, box 29/363 & 141.
158. DRO, ECA/11/2, Allotments Comm. report, 18 July 1941.
159. TC, group k, box 1/7; TC, group o, box 15/176.
160. TC, group o, box 22/no reference number; TC, group o, box 22/282.
161. TC, group o, box 17/187.
162. TC, group n, box 11; DRO, ECA/1/62, report 23 Sept. 1941.
163. DRO, ECA/1/62, report 17 Sept. 1941.
164. TC, group l, box 3/38.
165. TC, B1/7.
166. TC, group o, box 16/181.
167. TC, group o, box 16/181.
168. E&E, 27 Jan. 1945; TC, group o, box 18/203.
169. TC, group o, box 18/203; TC, group o, box 17/187.
170. TC, group n, box 14.
171. TC, group n, box 10.
172. ECA/Q, Exeter Soup Kitchen Comm. Minute Book, 1872–1941.
173. TC, group o, box 19/229.
174. TC, group o, box 22/266.
175. E&E, August 1943.
176. Longmate, *How we lived*, 141–2.
177. DRO, ECA/11/2, Allotments Comm. report, 5 Dec. 1941.
178. DRO, ECA/1/62, report 18 Dec. 1941.
179. TC, group o, box 19/146a.
180. TC, group o, box 22/260.
181. E&E, 1 Jan. 1942.
182. TC, group o, box 18/203; TC, group o, box 17/197.
183. TC, group o, box 21/260.
184. TC, group o, box 27/337.
185. DRO, ECA/1/63, report 9 Feb. 1942.
186. TC, group o, box 15/169.
187. TC, group o, box 17/197.
188. TC, group o, box 21/260; DRO, ECA/minute book vol. xxii, page 14.
189. TC, group o, box 20/no reference; TC, group o, box 22/279.
190. TC, group o, box 29/ARP misc; E&E, March 1942.
191. DRO, ECA/1/63, report 13 April 1942; TC, group K, box 1/7.
192. DRO, ECA/minute book vol. xxii, 17.
193. Thomas, *Fire*, 150–3.
194. TC, group n, box 12.
195. TC, group o, box 21/260.
196. TC, group o, box 19/229.
197. TC, group n, box 12.
198. E&E, 1 June 2004; *The Story of the Exeter Blitz*, 12.
199. TC, group L, box 7/71.
200. TC, group l, box 7.
201. TC, group m, box 9.
202. TC, group m, box 9/89.
203. TC, group k, box 2/25.
204. DRO, ECA/minute book vol. xxii, 19.
205. Davies, *Bombing of Exeter*, 9; Worrall, *Target Exeter*, 7; E&E, 5 May 1942.
206. DRO, 70/12.
207. DRO, ECA/1/63, report 9 June 1942.
208. TC, group o, box 20/232.
209. DRO, ECA/11/2, Allotments Comm. report, 13 June 1942.
210. DRO, ECA/1/63, report 3 June 1942.
211. TC, group o, box 29/198.
212. DRO, ECA/minute book vol. xxii, page 21.
213. DRO, TC, group k, box 2/18.
214. TC, group o, box 23, no reference.
215. TC, group o, box 15/176.
216. TC, group m, box 9.
217. TC, group k, box 2/16.
218. TC, group o, box 17/194.
219. TC, group o, box 18/203.
220. TC, group o, box 17/194.
221. TC, group k, box 8.
222. E&E, August 1942.
223. TC, group k, box 1/6.
224. TC, group k, box 2/25.
225. E&E, August 1942.
226. TC, group l, box 3/42.
227. Longmate, *How we lived*, 135.
228. TC, group o, box 17/188.
229. TC, group o, box 16/181.
230. E&E, Nov. 1945.
231. E&E, Nov. 1945.

232. TC, group o, box 18/203.
233. TC, group o, box 21/260.
234. TC, group m, box 6.
235. TC, group o, box 20/243.
236. TC, group o, box 18/203.
237. TC, group k, box 1/12.
238. TC, group o, box 22/cover of file missing.
239. TC, group o, box 18/207.
240. TC, group l, box 3/42.
241. TC, group l, box 3/42.
242. TC, group k, box 1/12.
243. TC, group o, box 20/249.
244. TC, group o, box 25/300.
245. TC, group o, box 18/203.
246. TC, group o, box 25/308.
247. DRO, ECA/1/63, report 26 Nov. 1942.
248. TC, group o, box 22/282.
249. DRO, ECA/minute book vol. xxii, 31.
250. TC, group k, box 2/25.
251. *E&E*, 23 Dec. 1942.
252. TC, group o, box 22/201; DRO, 1270C/YA1.
253. TC, group o, box 29/2. He died of a haemorrhage.
254. E&E, 1 Jan. 1943.
255. TC, group o, box 17/197.
256. DRO, ECA/11/2, Allotments Comm. report, 18 Jan.1943.
257. TC, group k, box 1, loose.
258. TC, group n, box 11.
259. TC, group o, box 19/217.
260. TC, group o, box 27/325.
261. E&E, 5 Jan. 1943.
262. TC, group o, box 26/42.
263. TC, group o, box 15/173.
264. TC, group o, box 21/260.
265. TC, group o, box 29/2.
266. TC, group o, box 19/229.
267. TC, group o, box 24/295.
268. TC, group o, box 25/301.
269. TC, group o, box 26/323.
270. *E&E*, 11 March 1943.
271. TC, group k, box 1/12.
272. TC, group o, box o/cover missing on file.
273. TC, group o, box 24/295.
274. DRO, ECA/minute book vol. xxii, 40.
275. TC, group o, box 16/182.
276. TC, group o, box 21/260.
277. TC, group o, box 26/318.
278. TC, group o, box 22/cover of file missing.
279. TC, group o, box 21/260.
280. TC, group o, box 24/295.
281. E&E, 28 Nov. 1942.
282. TC, group o, box 20/231.
283. TC, group o, box 18/203.
284. TC, group o, box 29/2.
285. TC, group k, box 1/12.
286. E&E, 1 June 1943.
287. TC, group o, box 15/173.
288. E&E, 4 & 5 June 1943.
289. TC, group o, box 22/cover of file missing.
290. DRO, ECA/11/2, Allotments Comm. report, 21 July 1943; TC, group o, box 18/203.
291. E&E, 24 July 1943.
292. TC, group m, box 8; TC, group k, box 2/18; TC, group o, box 17/188.
293. E&E, 24, 14 & 12 July 1943.
294. TC, group o, box 18/203.
295. E&E, 16 August 1943.
296. TC, group o, box 25/306; Longmate, *How we lived*, 135.
297. TC, group o, box 23/misc. folder.
298. TC, group o, box 27/338.
299. TC, group n, box 13.
300. DRO, ECA/minute book vol. xxii, 47.
301. TC, group m, box 6.
302. TC, group o, box 22/not referenced; TC, group o, box 20/not referenced.
303. TC, group m, box 6.
304. TC, group o, box 23/288.
305. TC, group o, box 23/290; TC, group o, box 16/182; TC, group l, box 3/42.
306. TC, group m, box 7.
307. E&E, 21 April 1945.
308. TC, group o, box 23/288.
309. DRO, ECA/20/1, misc. comm. minutes, Allied Services Club folder & group o, box 26/323.
310. TC, group o, box 27/untitled collection relating to Emergency Hospital Schemes.
311. TC, group o, box 26/323; TC, group o, box 26/231; TC, group o, box 26/323.
312. TC, group o, box 26/323; DRO, ECA/20/1, misc. comm. minutes, Allied Services Club folder.
313. TC, group o, box 25/306.
314. TC, group o, box 18/203.
315. TC, group o, box 19/229.
316. DRO, ECA/11/2, Allotments Comm. report, 1 Feb. 1944.
317. DRO, ECA/minute book vol. xxii, page 53.
318. TC, group o, box 26/323.
319. E&E, Feb. 1944.
320. E&E, 24 July 1943.
321. TC, group o, box 16/182.
322. TC, group o, box 25/301.
323. TC, group m, box 7/73.
324. TC, group o, box 26/323; *E&E*, March 1944.
325. TC, group o, box 27/military protected area, 1944.
326. TC, group m, box 6/69.
327. TC, group o, box 22/265.
328. TC, group o, box 26/323.
329. TC, group o, box 26/323.
330. DRO, ECA/11/2, Allotments Comm. report, 5 & 22 May 1944.

331. TC, group o, box 16/182.
332. TC, group o, box 18/203.
333. TC, group o, box 22/273.
334. TC, group o, box 26/323.
335. TC, group o, box 20/231.
336. TC, group o, box 18/203.
337. TC, group o, box 25/301.
338. TC, group o, box 27/file regarding accident of Mr R. A. Orchard.
339. TC, group o, box 18/203.
340. TC, group o, box 27/military protected area, 1944.
341. TC, group o, box 21/260.
342. TC, group o, box 21/260.
343. TC, group o, box 17/187.
344. TC, group o, box 23, no number; TC, group o, box 20/no reference.
345. TC, group o, box 29/2; TC, group o, box 18/203.
346. TC, group o, box 18/203; TC, group n, box 13.
347. TC, group k, box 2, 18; TC, group o, box 18/203.
348. TC, group o, box 21/260.
349. TC, group o, box 21/260.
350. TC, group o, box 19/225.
351. TC, group o, box 26/42 & group l, box 5/55.
352. Longmate, *How we lived*, 112.
353. TC, group o, box 23/290.
354. TC, group n, box 13.
355. TC, group o, box 20/231; E&E, 16 Dec. 1944.
356. TC, group o, box 18/203; TC, group n, box 11; TC, group o, box 16/181.
357. TC, group k, box 2/18.
358. E&E, 14, 28, 21 & 18 Dec. 1944, 6 Jan. 1945.
359. E&E, 2, 5, 13 & 24 Jan. 1945.
360. E&E, 18, 24, 5, 24, 25 & 27 Jan. 1945.
361. TC, group o, box 29/misc. correspondence.
362. TC, group o, box 26/323.
363. TC, group k, box 2/18.
364. E&E, 2 & 6 Feb. 1945.
365. E&E, 23 & 8 Feb. 1945.
366. TC, group k, box 2/18; TC, group o, box 17/188.
367. E&E, 31 March 1945.
368. E&E, 2, 7, 10, 13 & 22 March 1945.
369. E&E 18 April 1945; DRO, ECA/minute book vol. xxii, page 87; E&E, 28 April 1945.
370. TC, group o, box 23, misc. folder; E&E, 21 April 1945.
371. TC, group o, box 21/256.
372. E&E, 2& 17 April 1945.
373. E&E, 23 April 1945.
374. TC, group o, box 20/245; E&E, 8 May 1945.
375. TC, group o, box 21/260.
376. DRO, ECA/minute book vol. xxii, page 92; E&E, 16 May 1945.
377. E&E, 5 & 7 June 1945; TC, group k, box 1, loose.
378. TC, group o, box 29/misc. correspondence.
379. Longmate, *How we lived*, 47.
380. E&E, 26 July 1945.
381. E&E, 11, 14, 20, 13 & 3 July 1945.
382. E&E, 3 & 19 July 1945.
383. E&E, 1, 3, 4, 7, 9, 10, 11, 13, 15 & 18 August 1945.
384. E&E, 15, 18 August 1945.
385. E&E, 17 August 1945.
386. E&E, 3 Sept. 1945.
387. E&E, Nov. 1945 & 21 Sept 2004.
388. E&E, Nov. 1945; DRO, ECA/minute book vol. xxii, page 118.
389. DRO, ECA/minute book vol. xxii, page 159.
390. TC, group o, box 19/220; Longmate, *How we lived*, 47.
391. TC, group o, box 19/220.
392. TC, group o, box 19/220.
393. TC, group o, box 22/265.
394. Longmate, *How we lived*, 506; TC, group o, box 26/323.
395. DRO, ECA/minute book vol. xxii, page 136; TC, group k, box 2/20.
396. TC, group o, box 26/323.
397. TC, group o, box 27/332.
398. TC, group o, box 19/222.
399. TC, group o, box 0/29; TC, group o, box 19/146a.
400. TC, group o, box 18/202; TC, group o, box 22/280.
401. DRO, ECA/minute book vol. xxii, page 147; TC, group o, box 22/280.
402. TC, group o, box 27/328; TC, group o, box 16/182.
403. TC, group k, box 2/26.
404. TC, group 0, box 12.
405. Worrall, *Target Exeter*, 6.
406. Brierley, 'Exeter, 1939–74'; Venning, *Exeter*.
407. Todd Gray, *The Essence of Exeter* (Exeter, 2004), 5.
408. Todd Gray, *Lost Exeter* (Exeter, 2002).
409. These were the churches of St Mary Arches, St Stephen, St Lawrence and Bedford Chapel, 10–12 The Close, the hall of the Vicars Choral, Church Army House along with two adjacent properties, Bampfylde House, 15 to 120 Bedford Circus, St John's Hospital and School, Old Black Lion, Norman House and 166 Fore Street.

410. DRO, Engineer and Surveyor's Papers, box 76.

411. TC, group o, box 23/288.

412. J. Paton Watson and Patrick Abercrombie, *A Plan for Plymouth* (Plymouth, 1943).

413. E&E, 30 Nov. 1945; *New Chronicle*, 7 March 1946; Brierley, 'Exeter', 32.

414. Sharp, Exeter, 109, 87–8.

415. E&E, 6 March 1946; Gray, *Exeter Unveiled*, 101.

416. E&E, 20 Oct. 1948.

417. Brierley, 'Exeter', 16, 32, 34–5, 41, 170, 173–5, 184.

418. Venning, *Exeter*, 57–72; E&E, 18 Feb. 1949; *Western Morning News*, 23 Feb. 1949.

419. TC, group o, box 8.

420. Venning, *Exeter*, 77.

421. TC, group o, box 26/323; Venning, *Exeter*, 23, 83–7.

422. Venning, *Exeter*, 20–3; E&E, 5 Dec. 1946, 29 Sept. 1945, 4 Dec. 1945, 13 Sept. 1947.

423. E&E, 8 Jan. 1949.

424. *Western Morning News*, 17 Jan. 1950; E&E, 29 Dec. 1949; Venning, *Exeter*, 27–8, 44; DRO, ECA/minute Book vol. xxii, 251.

425. Hugh Meller, *Exeter Architecture* (1989), 69.

426. E&E, 4 August 1944.

427. Todd Gray, *Lost Devon* (Exeter, 2004), 22.

428. E&E, 2 March 1946.

Index